THE LOGIC OF EQUALITY

If you are to deceive someone else and to avoid deception yourself, you must know precisely the respects in which things are similar and dissimilar to one another.
Socrates in Plato's *Phaedrus*

The Logic of Equality
A Formal Analysis of Non-Discrimination Law

ERIC HEINZE
University of London, Queen Mary

Routledge
Taylor & Francis Group

LONDON AND NEW YORK

First published 2003 by Ashgate Publishing

Reissued 2018 by Routledge
2 Park Square, Milton Park, Abingdon, Oxon OX14 4RN
711 Third Avenue, New York, NY 10017, USA

Routledge is an imprint of the Taylor & Francis Group, an informa business

Publisher's Note
The publisher has gone to great lengths to ensure the quality of this reprint but points out that some imperfections in the original copies may be apparent.

Disclaimer
The publisher has made every effort to trace copyright holders and welcomes correspondence from those they have been unable to contact.

A Library of Congress record exists under LC control number: 2003045330

ISBN 13: 978-1-138-71555-4 (hbk)
ISBN 13: 978-1-315-19748-7 (ebk)

Contents

Series Preface

The objective of the Applied Legal Philosophy series is to publish work which adopts a theoretical approach to the study of particular areas or aspects of law or deals with general theories of law in a way which focuses on issues of practical moral and political concern in specific legal contexts.

In recent years there has been an encouraging tendency for legal philosophers to utilize detailed knowledge of the substance and practicalities of law and a noteworthy development in the theoretical sophistication of much legal research. The series seeks to encourage these trends and to make available studies in law which are both genuinely philosophical in approach and at the same time based on appropriate legal knowledge and directed towards issues in the criticism and reform of actual laws and legal systems.

The series will include studies of all the main areas of law, presented in a manner which relates to the concerns of specialist legal academics and practitioners. Each book makes an original contribution to an area of legal study while being comprehensible to those engaged in a wide variety of disciplines. Their legal content is principally Anglo-American, but a wide-ranging comparative approach is encouraged and authors are drawn from a variety of jurisdictions.

Tom D. Campbell
Series Editor
Centre for Applied Philosophy and Public Ethics
Charles Sturt University, Canberra

Abbreviations

AJDA	*Actualité juridique, droit administrative*
All ER	*All England Reports*
BverfGE	*Entscheidungen des Bundesverfassungsgerichts*
CE	Conseil d'Etat (France)
Dalloz	*Recueil Dalloz*
ECHR	European Convention on Human Rights
Eur. Ct. H.R. (ser. A)	*Publications of the European Court of Human Rights, Series A*
GG	Grundgesetz (Germany)
GW	Grondwet (Netherlands)
HR	Hoge Raad (Netherlands)
ICCPR	International Covenant on Civil and Political Rights
NJ	*Nederlandse Jurisprudentie*
UDHR	Universal Declaration of Human Rights
UN Doc.	United Nations Document
UNGA	United Nations General Assembly
UNTS	*United Nations Treaty Series*
US	*United States Reports*

Introduction

"Human rights is the idea of our time, the only political-moral idea that has received universal acceptance."[1] Louis Henkin's questionable proclamation does have a point: traditional civil rights and liberties have been enshrined in many national constitutions and international treaties—sometimes with no effect, sometimes with striking success. Of course, no two rights instruments are identical. The United States Bill of Rights was drafted in 1791, with a mere ten tersely worded provisions.[2] Only six have regularly been invoked with success.[3] By contrast, two centuries later, the International Covenant on Civil and Political Rights[4] included 27 substantive articles, several drafted in considerable detail.[5]

Despite such differences, a common core of rights can be found in virtually all instruments. That core might be said to include protections from cruel or degrading treatment, rights to a fair trial, rights of free expression or belief, or equal protection of the laws.[6] But how common is that core? Many instruments contain words like "degrading treatment," "fair trial" or "equal protection." Yet such words can be interpreted differently in different jurisdictions. Consider a State in which a norm is legally adopted but not enforced. Shall we say that, in that State, the norm is literally meaningless? That would be odd. It is common for a government whose laws prohibit torture nevertheless to torture people. We might well point to such a regime as evidence that the norm against torture is ineffective, but not as evidence that the norm has no meaning. Shall we instead say that, although the norm in that State is meaningful, its meaning is ignored? But then what *is* that meaning? Do rights retain any necessary and fixed meanings, valid for all legal systems in which they appear?

---

[1] Henkin 1990: ix.

[2] U.S. Const. amends. I – X. The number of US constitutional rights is increased through other constitutional provisions, such as the protection of writs of habeas corpus, U.S. Const. art. I, § 9, cl. 2, or the prohibition of ex post facto laws, U.S. Const. art. I, § 9, cl. 3. See also U.S. Const. amends. XIII, XIV, XV, XIX, XXIV, XXVI. On the further recognition of rights through judicial construction, see, e.g., Nowak and Rotunda, 2000: ch. 11.

[3] See, e.g., Nowak and Rotunda, 2000: ch. 10.

[4] 999 U.N.T.S. 171 (*entered into force*, Mar. 23, 1976).

[5] But see Human Rights Committee, General Comment 23, U.N. Doc. HRI\GEN\1\Rev.1 at 38 (1994) (noting procedural limitations on the justiciability of art. 1).

[6] See, e.g., Robertson and Merrills, 1996: 2-7.

The example considered in this book will be the non-discrimination norm. Compare the following formulations,

(a)   According to Article 14 of the European Convention on Human Rights, "[t]he enjoyment of the rights and freedoms set forth in this Convention will be secured without discrimination on any ground such as sex, race, colour, language, religion, political or other opinion, national or social origin, association with a national minority, birth or other status."[7]

(b)   According to article 3 of the German Basic Law, "(1) Everyone is equal before the law. (2) Men and women have equal rights. [...]; (3) No burden will be imposed, nor any benefit conferred, on anyone on the basis of his sex, family origin, race, language, homeland or origin, creed or religious or political beliefs. [...]"[8]

(c)   According to the Fourteenth Amendment of the United States Constitution, "[n]o State shall . . . deny to any person within its jurisdiction the equal protection of the laws."[9]

Are passages (a), (b) and (c) merely three ways of saying the same thing?[10] Do similar terms appearing in different legal instruments imply similarities in

---

[7] Convention for the Protection of Human Rights and Fundamental Freedoms, art. 14, 213 U.N.T.S. 222 (*entered into force*, 3 Sept. 1953), as amended by Protocols 3, 5, 8 and 11 (*entered into force*, 21 Sept. 1970, 20 Dec. 1971, 1 Jan. 1990 and 1 Nov. 1998, respectively).

[8] GG art. 3. ("(1) Alle Menschen sind vor dem Gesetz gleich. (2) Männer und Frauen sind gleichberechtigt. [...] (3) Niemand darf wegen seines Geschlechtes, seiner Abstammung, seiner Rasse, seiner Sprache, seiner Heimat und Herkunft, seines Glaubens, seiner religiösen oder politischen Anschauungen benachteiligt oder bevorzugt werden. [...]")

[9] U.S. Const. amend. XIV, §1.

[10] As we will be concerned with language, note that the concluding paragraph to the European Convention provides that the English and French texts are equally authentic. The French text of article 14 reads as follows,

La jouissance des droits et libertés reconnus dans la présente Convention doit être assurée, sans distinction aucune, fondée notamment sur le sexe, la race, la couleur, la langue, la religion, les opinions politiques ou toutes autres opinions, l'origine nationale ou sociale, l'appartenance à une minorité nationale, la fortune, la naissance ou toute autre situation.

It can be argued that locutions such as "doit être assurée" or "toute autre situation" provide a stronger version than their English counterparts, although that discrepancy has not yet given rise to significant problems of interpretation by the Strasbourg bodies. On the phrase "doit être assurée," cf. the case "Relating to Certain Aspects of the Laws on the Use of Languages in Education in Belgium," 6 Eur. Ct. H.R. 305 (ser. A) (1968) [hereinafter *Belgian Linguistic* case], and Harris *et al.* 1995: 463. On "toute autre situation," cf. van Dijk & van Hoof 1998: 719. Note that we will also be examining some sex discrimination cases brought

meaning? Do different terms imply different meanings? How would we decide? With multilingual dictionaries? Through comparative empirical studies? But what would it mean for cases to be "comparable"? Is discrimination against Hispanics in Los Angeles "comparable" to discrimination against Turks in Hamburg?

We might compare (a), (b) and (c) by examining explanations of them promulgated, respectively, by the final authoritative bodies charged with their interpretation,

(a') According to the European Court of Human Rights, a difference of treatment is discriminatory if it has "no objective and reasonable justification."[11]

(b') According to the German Constitutional Court (*Bundesverfassungsgericht*), there is discrimination when "one group of persons subject to the [non-discrimination] norm is treated differently from other persons subject to the norm, although there exists between the two groups no differences of such a kind or of such a degree that unequal treatment could be justified."[12]

(c') According to the United States Supreme Court, "[t]he Equal Protection Clause of the Fourteenth Amendment . . . is essentially a direction that all persons similarly situated should be treated alike."[13]

In other words, we might try to compare the norms in (a), (b) and (c) by comparing the interpretative statements in (a'), (b') and (c'). Yet that latter task would raise questions of its own. How have those statements been applied in practice? Have the courts made any other relevant pronouncements? Is there any other relevant law, e.g., in the form of statute or treaty?

But let us leave those larger questions to one side. For argument's sake, let us assume (a'), (b') and (c') to be distinctly authoritative. We are still left with the problem that, in order to compare (a'), (b') and (c'), we would have to compare the meanings of their decisive terms: "alike," "objective," "reasonable," "justified." Legal theory has long taught that such terms cannot yield certain meanings even within a legal system, let alone across systems.[14] Throughout the world, we can

---

under European Union law before the European Court of Justice, pursuant to Council Directive 76/207/EEC, 1976 O.J. (L 39/40). Article 2(1) of the Directive provides that "there shall be no discrimination whatsoever on grounds of sex either directly or indirectly . . . ."

[11] *Belgian Linguistic* case, 6 Eur. Ct. H.R. (ser. A) at 34.

[12] 95 BVerfGE 143, 154-55 (1996) ("eine Gruppe von Normadressaten im Vergleich zu anderen Normadressaten anders behandelt [wird], obwohl zwischen beiden Gruppen keine Unterschiede von solcher Art und solchem Gewicht bestehen, daß sie die ungleiche Behandlung rechtfertigen könnten") (internal citations omitted).

[13] City of Cleburne v. Cleburne Living Center, Inc., 473 U.S. 432, 439 (1985).

[14] See, e.g., Fletcher, 1996: ch. 3; Cotterrell, 1989: chs. 6 – 7; Kelman, 1987.

find legal instruments containing a non-discrimination norm; but it is questionable whether we can find any definitive, non-platitudinous statement of that norm's content which would be shared by all of them. (The same can be said of other norms.[15] In this book, the non-discrimination norm will serve only as an example, albeit an important one, as many theorists have maintained that the concept of equality—like treatment of like cases—is presupposed by the very idea of a system of rules or the rule of law.[16])

Although introduced as a study in comparative law, the problem is principally about the determinacy of a legal concept. (This book can be called a study in comparative law to the extent that it proposes a formal model applicable to all regimes, *despite* institutional or jurisprudential differences. Insofar as it departs from the empiricism of most comparative law, it can be called a study in non-empirical comparativism.) "Like treatment of like" is the age-old maxim, but who's to say what "like" means? If I treat a man and a woman differently, am I treating likes unalike? Or unalikes unalike? Is it sometimes right to treat likes unalike or unalikes alike?

The problem of determinacy in legal norms is commonly approached through theories of open texture. In Hart's words,

> Whichever device, precedent or legislation, is chosen for the communication of standards of behaviour, these, however smoothly they work over the great mass of ordinary cases, will, at some point where their application is in question, prove indeterminate; they will have what has been termed an *open texture*.[17]

Theories of open texture have been developed by scholars from legal realism and the *Freirechtsschule*, through analytic positivism, liberalism, critical legal studies, deconstructionism and post-modernism. For most of those theories, open texture remains something grey and murky—even for Dworkin, whose "one answer" may indeed be the right one, but is not thereby obvious or uncontroversial.[18] This book seeks neither to eliminate open texture (that is impossible) nor to review the wealth of theories about it, but to propose a "science" of indeterminacy: a method of formal analysis aimed at pinpointing elements of determinacy underlying the open texture of a legal norm. No prior training in logic will be assumed, since the requisite concepts are explained as the analysis progresses.

---

[15] See Heinze, 2003a.

[16] "The rule of law . . . implies the precept that similar cases be treated similarly. Men could not regulate their actions by means of rules if this precept were not followed." Rawls, 1999: 208. Cf., e.g., Aristotle, 1941a: 1006-07; Kelsen, 1960: 390-97. Despite that wide sweep of the concept of equality, this study will concentrate on non-discrimination norms as applied within regimes of individual civil rights and liberties. But for a broader formulation, cf. Section 14.5 *infra*.

[17] Hart, 1961: 124 (original emphasis).

[18] Cf. Dworkin, 1977: 110-23; 1986: 238-50.

We will see how indeterminacy in the non-discrimination norm already presupposes elements that are fixed and determinate. We will see that the sheer existence of controversy about the substantive clarity or ambiguity of the norm already presupposes some level of formal determinacy. This book will serve to illustrate the broader point that controversial or open-ended elements of legal discourse are commonly constrained by determinate, formal elements. We will see that decisive components of the non-discrimination norm maintain a fixed and determinate structure both within and across legal systems, regardless of differences or uncertainties about the norm's substantive content.

Method and Overview

Logical analysis of law has long aroused suspicion. Many have doubted whether a strictly formal model can illuminate the subtler or more controversial elements of legal reasoning. Holmes insisted that "a page of history is worth a volume of logic."[19] Yet logical analyses have made considerable progress in recent years. Three distinct approaches have emerged. The first and oldest draws upon traditional logic: legal argument is analyzed with reference to syllogistic structures familiar from classical logic. Once maligned as "mechanical," the versatility of that approach has again drawn attention.[20] The second approach involves deontic logic, which sets forth relationships among concepts of obligation, permission, and prohibition.[21] The third approach, and the most influential in Anglo-American scholarship, is Hohfeldian analysis.[22] Hohfeld found that the one word "right" was being used in ways so divergent as to produce errors in legal reasoning. He sought to ascertain distinctions among such concepts as "claim", "privilege," "power" or "immunity." Subsequent scholars have refined Hohfeld's system and made it central to analytic jurisprudence.[23] Those three approaches have not been mutually exclusive. Some scholars have wedded deontic and Hohfeldian approaches;[24] and the traditional approach commonly hovers in the background of deontic and Hohfeldian analyses.[25]

More recently, I have proposed a fourth approach, which is largely followed in this book. In *The Logic of Liberal Rights*, I proposed a formal analysis aimed at ascertaining six "background theories" which underlie legal argument in disputes about civil rights and liberties.[26] While that book provided a general account of

---

[19] New York Trust Co. v. Eisner, 256 U.S. 345, 349 (1921) (Holmes, J.).
[20] See, e.g., Meier, 2000; Rodes and Pospesel, 1997; Soeteman, 1989.
[21] See Kalinowski, 1972; von Wright, 1963; 1951.
[22] Hohfeld, 1946.
[23] For a brief bibliography of representative studies, see Simmonds, 2001: xxviii-xxix.
[24] See, e.g, Sumner, 1987: ch. 2.
[25] Cf. Saunders, 1990 (proposing a fully formalised account of Hohfeldian analysis).
[26] See also Heinze, 2004; 2003b.

civil rights and liberties, this one examines only the non-discrimination norm, insofar as the concept of equality raises distinct structural issues. This book assumes no familiarity with *The Logic of Liberal Rights*.

This book is not a general introduction to law and logic. Its only purpose is to answer the question initially posed: does the non-discrimination norm have any fixed components which remain constant both within and across jurisdictions? The analysis will examine general points of logic only to the extent that they serve to answer that question. Some techniques in this book would not be found in standard textbooks on logic. That is not because the analysis contradicts any basic postulates of logic, but because it seeks to elicit specific features of non-discrimination law.

The cases are drawn from the United States, Germany, the European Union and the European Convention on Human Rights. No familiarity with those systems, or with any of the cases arising under them, will be assumed. The inclusion of cases from the United States will be of particular interest, as US non-discrimination jurisprudence, with its reliance on the complex judicial standards promulgated by the Supreme Court,[27] departs markedly from the approaches found under other contemporary international, regional or national regimes.[28] US courts, unlike their non-US counterparts, almost never examine the methods deployed in other legal systems, thus reinforcing the impression of a self-sufficient regime, and raising all the more forcefully the question whether a model purporting to fit all regimes applies even to such an aberrant and insulated one.[29]

A summary of the contents is as follows. In Parts I, II and III, constituent elements of the formal model are introduced. In Part IV, those elements are combined to generate the basic categories of argument in discrimination law.

Part I begins with the concept of *treatment*. After a survey of preliminary issues in chapter 1, chapter 2 distinguishes between *factual* and *normative* assertions about treatment, and between assertions of *equal* and *unequal* treatment. In chapter 3, a technique is introduced whereby assertions about treatment are used as a basis for deriving further assertions at a higher level of generality. Chapter 4 undertakes a more thorough study of normative assertions about treatment. Chapter 5 introduces a means by which the formal values of symbols can be defined economically in terms of other symbols. Chapter 6 provides an overview of the ways in which formal assertions about treatment are

---

[27] See Section 14.4 *infra*. Cf. Heinze, 2003b.

[28] The margin of appreciation doctrine promulgated by the European Court of Human Rights is arguably of similar complexity. It has not, however, been applied to non-discrimination cases, which, instead, have used the "objective and reasonable justification" standard noted above in (a').

[29] While the standard lexicon of US non-discrimination jurisprudence is not fully incompatible with that of non-US jurisdictions, reconciliation is only possible in rather general terms, and certainly provides no guarantee of similar resolutions to similar disputes, particularly in controversial cases. See, e.g., Heringa, 1999: 25.

constructed. In chapter 7, factual assertions and assertions arguments are conjoined to form *compound assertions* about treatment.

In Part II, we examine the proposition that discrimination disputes concern the assignment of some individual to a larger class of individuals sharing an *objective status*, such as race, ethnicity, religion, language or sex. Arguments about objective status are examined in conjunction with arguments about treatment. In chapter 8, the earlier factual assertions about treatment are refined so as to incorporate assertions about objective status. In chapter 9, the earlier normative assertions are refined to incorporate assertions about objective status. In chapter 10, the revised factual and normative assertions are again combined to generate compound assertions, encompassing assertions about objective status.

In Part III, it is suggested that, in conjunction with arguments about objective status, discrimination disputes include arguments about *subjective merit—* individual determinations of need, interest or ability. In chapters 11 and 12, the factual and normative arguments which had been refined in Part Two to include objective status are further refined to include the element of subjective merit. Chapter 13, we reach the final form for the general kinds of arguments arising in discrimination discourse.

In Part IV, those general forms of argument are elaborated and combined to generate the four basic types of discrimination disputes. Chapter 14 examines the *traditional* model, which covers many of the more familiar kinds of cases. Chapter 15 examines the *impact* model, which arises in disputes about unintentional or *de facto* discrimination. Chapter 16 introduces *accommodation* disputes, arising from allegations of failure to undertake measures to meet an individual's special needs or requirements. Chapter 17 concludes with a *non-recognition* model, corresponding to denials by an accused party that a claim of objective status provides a cognizable basis for a claim.

The ideas in this book were presented at the 1998 International Conference on Comparative Non-Discrimination Law, at the University of Utrecht. I am grateful to the organizers Titia Loenen and Peter Rodriquez for their cooperation, and to Rikki Holtmaat for her contributions in chairing a helpful session. Valuable comments were also provided by Tom Wormgoor. In addition, I would like to thank Tom Campbell, John Irwin and the staff at Ashgate. Unless otherwise indicated, translations of foreign materials are mine, and are not official.

Eric Heinze
University of London, Queen Mary

Part I

Treatment

1 Preliminary Concepts

In this chapter, we adopt basic symbols to represent the *parties* to disputes, in order to develop a preliminary means of expressing arguments.

1.1 The Contentious Case

In this book, discrimination is examined only within the context of contentious cases[1]—law suits brought by one party against another within a judicial[2] forum. That approach might appear to neglect non-confrontational processes, such as negotiation or alternative dispute resolution. However, the fact that the framework is conflictual does not mean that the parties to a dispute are precluded from friendly settlement, which may still proceed in the shadow of prospective litigation. In that case, the background structures of argument, as developed in this study, would remain intact.

Readers from civil-law traditions may suspect that the focus on contentious cases assumes a common-law bias, disproportionately emphasizing the judicial function. However, the analysis will treat contentious cases only as examples of rights balancing, without regard to the legal status of judicial holdings in any given jurisdiction. Questions of judicial precedent will assume no special role. By the end of the book, it will perhaps be clear that the same general forms of argument arising from the non-discrimination norm structure debate in other fora, such as legislative or administrative bodies, or civil-law courts not observing formal principles of *stare decisis*, as well as the kinds of debates which arise within the public at large.

---

[1] In view of the focus on arguments adduced in substantive rights disputes, the corpus to be examined includes only judgments on the merits of disputes, without reference to issues of procedure or jurisdiction. Arguments will be drawn from published judgments, even, in some cases, if they differ from the parties' original oral or written submissions; and even if those submissions themselves change over the course of litigation. A broader corpus, embracing written or oral pleadings, or decisions of lower courts or bodies, would provide further instances for applying the model, but in no way bears upon its structure.

[2] The analysis would apply equally to quasi-judicial bodies such as the Human Rights Committee of the United Nations, constituted under ICCPR article 28, and authorised to receive individual complaints under the First Optional Protocol to the International Covenant on Civil and Political Rights, 999 UNTS 302 (*entered into force*, 23 Mar. 1976).

1.2   Parties

This book is concerned with arguments made or presupposed by parties in contentious cases. Questions about the meanings of statements, and the ways and contexts in which they are made, pose difficult problems in logical and semantic analysis. We will take some simplifying steps, which will create no difficulties as long as it is borne in mind that they apply only within the confines of the model, and are not intended to express broader facts about language, logic, law or legal discourse.

Consider an example. Regimes assign to disputing parties different names at various stages of litigation: plaintiff and defendant, *requérant* and *défendeur*, *Kläger* and *Beklagte*. Even within one system, various names appear, depending on the type, or stage, of the litigation: plaintiff, defendant, appellant, respondent, petitioner. For many practical or analytical purposes, there might be good reasons for maintaining those differences. However, for the limited purposes of our model, they will be set aside. Parties complaining of discrimination, regardless of the jurisdiction in which, or the stage of litigation at which, their complaint is brought, will be called *claimants*. Defending parties will be called *respondents*. We will adopt the following two axioms. They may seem trivial, but will come in handy in the next section,

Claimant Axiom: Every claimant seeks a finding that a non-discrimination norm has been violated.

Respondent Axiom: Every respondent seeks a finding that a non-discrimination norm has *not* been violated.

Claimants will be denoted by the upper-case Roman letter A, respondents by the letter Z. Where reference need simply be made to some *party*, without specification as to whether that party is the claimant (A) or the respondent (Z), the lower-case Greek letter theta (θ) will be used. The letter θ thus represents any entity bringing or defending a claim, which, depending on a given jurisdiction's standing rules, may be one individual, several individuals, an organization, a corporation or a government body.

The relationship between A, Z and θ shows that some symbols can be defined in terms of other symbols. *Postulates* (Ps) will be introduced to serve that function, with the aid of the symbol "$\subset$". In order to state that A or Z are possible values of θ, we will adopt the following "θ postulate,"

$$Ps(\theta) \quad \theta \subset A, Z$$

As the analysis progresses, additional symbols and postulates will be introduced. For reference, they are compiled in the Appendix.

1.3   Assertions and Positions

What does a party to a dispute *say*? Lawyers, or their strategies, may change.
Some lawyers may be inarticulate. In some jurisdictions, submissions may be both
oral and written, and inconsistencies may arise within or across them, particularly
when litigation proceeds over a long period. A court may adopt views not adduced
by either party, including a view favorable to a party which that party did not in fact
express. Note also that, when developing a model, we are concerned with
generality: not only with actual arguments made in actual cases, but also with
hypothetical arguments imaginable for actual and possible cases.

This book examines appellate-level cases, where, for the most part, the
parties' overall submissions have already been stipulated. Nevertheless, the formal
model is intended to anticipate the widest variety of arguments. That is where the
Claimant and Respondent Axioms adopted in the last section will help. It will be
accepted that parties are not always clear or consistent in their submissions.
However, an outer limit will be drawn: we will stipulate (although we know that
there may in practice be the occasional blunder): (1) that no claimant makes an
argument asserting or presupposing that a non-discrimination norm *has not* been
violated; and (2) that no respondent makes an argument asserting or presupposing
that a non-discrimination norm *has* been violated.

Accordingly, the term *assertion* will be used (1') to denote a statement
adduced by, attributed to, or attributable to a *claimant* in support of a claim that a
non-discrimination norm *has* been violated; or (2') to denote a statement adduced
by, attributed to, or attributable to a respondent in support of a claim that a non-
discrimination norm *has not* been violated.[3] Examples of such assertions are
"Treatment in this case is unequal" or "Treatment in this case should be equal."
The analysis will be devoted to examining the structure of such assertions and their
inter-relationships. The term *position* will be defined as *a set of one or more
assertions adduced by a party*. The claimant's position will be called an *A position*.
For example, to say that A makes assertion *p*, we write,

A: *p*

The respondent's position will be called a *Z position*. We can say that Z adduces
some assertion *q*,

Z: *q*

Accordingly, a *θ position* represents either an A position or a Z position. To say
that *some party* asserts *x*, we write,

θ: *x*

---

[3] For examination of the ascription of statements to parties, including problems of opaque
contexts or propositional attitudes, see Heinze, 2003a: secs. 3.1–3.3.

1.4   Hierarchy and Substitution

The relationships among the symbols A, Z and θ can be illustrated by means of a simple tree diagram,

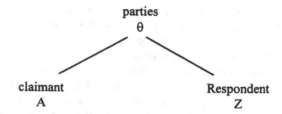

That diagram illustrates a hierarchy of relationships among the symbols. We will say that one symbol is *hierarchically inferior* to another (which is *hierarchically superior*) when the inferior symbol represents only one of several possible values of the superior one. For example, the claimant (A) represents only one kind of party (θ). It is therefore hierarchically inferior to the symbol θ. Of course, those concepts of hierarchical superiority and inferiority contain no normative content. They do not refer to more or less powerful or important actors, but only to broader or narrower classes of symbols.

A hierarchically superior symbol can always substitute for any inferior symbol. For example, the position A: p can be translated as,

"The claimant asserts p."

That position implies the position θ: p,

"Some party asserts p."

Ordinarily, we would prefer to use the formula A: p. Being hierarchically inferior, it is more precise. Nevertheless, as the analysis proceeds, it will sometimes be useful to write formulas at higher levels of abstraction.

1.5   Translation

It is important to have reliable ways of translating between symbolic expressions and natural language. Consider a dispute in which it is alleged that an individual, Croft, has been a target of discrimination. Croft might argue A: p, where p represents a statement such as "I have been unfairly treated." If the complaint were brought by some other party on Croft's behalf, a more accurate translation would refer to Croft in the grammatical third person: "*She* has been unfairly treated." Similarly, Croft might be only one of a larger group of individuals, perhaps even a class action. The argument A: *p* might then best be translated "*We* have been unfairly treated." In this study, the facts of the case will ordinarily be clear enough to indicate an accurate translation.

Ordinary language includes still further elements which we will disregard for purposes of translation into symbolic language. For example, differences in verb tense might produce different translations: "Croft asserts *p*," "Croft asserted *p*," "Croft had asserted *p*." Or consider combinations of verbs with adverbs: "Croft ardently asserted *p*," "Croft cleverly asserted *p*." Those differences, too, will have no affect on the model. Where such locutions arise in the exercise sets, the point will be to learn to disregard them, and to translate them exactly as you would translate "The claimant asserts *p*."[4]

Exercise Set 1-1

Translate the following statements into symbolic form. (Answers to the Exercise Sets appear at the end of each chapter.)

Example: The claimant asserts x.
Answer: A: x

1. On behalf of Lara, the respondent asserts x.
2. The claimants repeatedly insisted on y.
3. Yet the respondents had always conceded y.
4. Someone will no doubt proffer p.

1.6 Logical Operators

Statements are rarely meaningful in isolation. Logical *operators*[5] are tools used for stating relationships among statements in unambiguous form. In this book, we will use three operators: the *negation* ("not"), the *conjunction* ("and") and the *conditional* ("if…, then…").[6] One of the principal functions of standard logic is to

---

[4] For fuller examination of the role of verb tenses and of modal, conditional and counterfactual statements as expressed in θ positions, see Heinze, 2003a: sec. 3.4.
[5] These are known also as "propositional operators" or "propositional connectives." See, e.g., Detlefsen *et al.*, 1999: 85.
[6] Those familiar with formal logic may be surprised that no use is made of disjunctions. Certainly, if the model set forth here were to be incorporated into a calculus for validity testing, the role of disjunctions would have to be considered. While a disjunctive operator could be introduced into the model developed in this book, that would create several

test arguments for their validity. For that purpose, detailed attention must be paid to the precise meanings of operators (those meanings being ascertained, for example, by means of truth tables). Our aims, however, will be different. The problems relative to testing the validity of arguments will not be a major concern. We will be able to rely on ordinary, common-sense meanings of "not," "and" or "if..., then...," without having to worry about logical fallacies arising.

One operation, then, is *negation*. We will say that one statement negates another when the two cannot both be true.[7] The negating function will be denoted by a symbol called a "tilde" (~) appearing before the symbol representing the negated statement. If p represents a statement, then $\sim p$ represents the negation, e.g.,

A: p *The claimant asserts that treatment is equal.*

A: $\sim p$ *The claimant asserts that treatment is **not** equal.*

Economy of notation is preferable, but there is no theoretical limit to the number of times an assertion can be negated. A *double negation* is not uncommon,

A: $\sim\!\!\sim p$ *The claimant asserts that treatment is **not unequal**.*

For any statement p, we will say that p is identical to $\sim\!\!\sim p$,[8]

$$p = \sim\!\!\sim p$$

Accordingly, we will say that the position A: $\sim\!\!\sim p$ means the same thing as A: p. Similarly, the position A: $\sim\!\!\sim\!\!\sim p$ means the same thing as A: ~p, and so forth.

A *conjunction* is a combination of statements which is true when each individual statement is true.[9] For example, the conjunctive statement "John has an apple and Mary has an orange" is true when it is true that John has an apple, and that Mary has an orange. In the same way, the statement "John has an apple, but Mary has an orange" is true when it is true that John has an apple and that Mary has an orange. The conjunction will be represented by a dot (·), which we will normally read as "and" (but which can also be read as "but," "however," "yet,"

---

complications, without adding much insight into the non-discrimination norm. For further analysis, see Heinze, 2003a: sec. 5.4.

[7] More precisely, negation "[s]ignifies either an operator that is used to negate the truth of propositions or a compound proposition formed by applying such an operator to a proposition." Detlefsen *et al.*, 1999: 72.

[8] Strictly speaking, while it would be accurate to represent p and $\sim\!\!\sim p$ in a biconditional relationship, the question of identity is more complex. Within the confines of the present analysis, a relationship of identity can be stipulated without difficulties cropping up later on.

[9] See, e.g., Detlefsen *et al.*, 1999: 24.

"nevertheless," "despite," or some similar locution.)[10] Accordingly, in order to express the sentence "the claimant asserts p and q," we will write,

A: $p \cdot q$

A *conditional* relationship is a combination of two statements about which it is asserted that *if* one of them is true, *then* the other is true. That relationship is commonly denoted by an arrow ($\rightarrow$)[11] placed between two symbols representing the statements. Thus in order to express the claimant's view that q is the case *if p* is the case, we would write,

A: $p \rightarrow q$

In that construction, the term preceding the arrow is commonly called the *antecedent*, and the term following the arrow is commonly called the *consequent*.[12]

Exercise Set 1-2

Translate into symbolic form.

Example: The claimant asserts p.
Answer: A: p

1.   The respondent emphatically denied p.
2.   Some party embraced p and q.
3.   The claimant argued that x was true if y was true.
4.   Some party insisted that, if x is not true, then y is true.

---

[10] In traditional logic (in contrast to theories of ordinary language, e.g., Grice 1975), conjunctions such as "but," "however," "yet," "nevertheless" or "despite" provide no more than rhetorical variations of the word "and." In each case, the conjoined assertions are equally asserted to be true: the statement "*p* and *q*" and the statement "*p* but *q*" both equally assert *p* and *q*. The statement "The sun is shining *and* the wind is blowing" and the statement "The sun is shining *but* the wind is blowing" both assert that: (1) the sun is shining, and (2) the wind is blowing. Words other than "and" might convey a substantively different meaning if used elliptically, such as to imply not only that the sun is shining and the wind is blowing, but also that the wind does not generally blow when the sun is shining. That proposition, however, cannot be inferred strictly from the statement "The sun is shining but the wind is blowing." It can derive only from the addition of a premise such as, "The wind does not generally blow when the sun shines," so as to create a proposition of the form "*p* and *q* and *r*": "The sun is shining, *and* the wind is blowing, *and* the wind does not generally blow when the sun shines." See, e.g., Rodes and Pospesel, 1997: 19-20.
[11] See, e.g., Detlefsen, 1999: 114.
[12] *Id.*

Answers to Exercises

Exercise Set 1-1

1. Z: x
3. Z: y

2. A: y
4. θ: p

Exercise Set 1-2

1. Z: ~p
3. A: y → x

2. θ: p · q
4. θ: ~x → y

2 The Basic Treatment Symbols

From its origins in a more strictly *de jure* concept of equal protection before the law, the range of circumstances under which discrimination claims may be brought has broadened in recent decades. Contemporary non-discrimination jurisprudence has increasingly embraced issues such as *de facto* discriminatory impact, or affirmative action, or special accommodation.[1] We must therefore develop a broad concept of "treatment," which can account for a wide variety of claims. However, we will not begin by examining a great number of cases. In fact, for the next few chapters, we will examine just one case, extracting from it as much formal structure as we can, before proceeding to examine other kinds of disputes.

2.1 *Dothard v. Rawlinson*

In this and the next few chapters, in order to develop some of the basic components of the model, we will examine the US case of *Dothard v. Rawlinson*.[2] On its facts, the case certainly has some interesting and unusual features. As a formal matter, however, we will see that it is a very typical case.

These are its facts. Dianne Rawlinson was a 22-year old woman who had completed a major course of university study in correctional psychology. She submitted an application for employment as a prison guard to the Board of Corrections of the State of Alabama. Her application was rejected on the grounds that she had failed to meet the minimum weight requirement of 120 pounds. Claiming that the height and weight requirements discriminated against women (women being on average shorter and lighter than men), she brought a complaint of sex discrimination against the State authorities under federal anti-discrimination legislation.[3] She argued that the height and weight requirements, albeit facially neutral, excluded over 41% of women applicants, while excluding less than 1% of men.[4] While her suit was pending, the Alabama Board of Corrections adopted further regulations excluding women from duty in all-male prisons as guards in contact positions with inmates. Those positions were described, in part, as follows,

---

[1] See chapters 14-17 *infra*.
[2] 433 U.S. 321 (1977).
[3] Title VII of the Civil Rights Act of 1964, as amended, 42 USC §§ 2000e et seq. and 42 USC §1983.
[4] 433 U.S. at 329-30.

A. [...] [T]he presence of the opposite sex would cause disruption to the orderly running and security of the institution.

B. [...] [T]he position would require contact with the inmates of the opposite sex without the presence of others.

C. [...] [T]he position would require patrolling dormitories, restrooms, or showers [...]

D. [...] [T]he position would require search of inmates of the opposite sex ....[5]

Rawlinson amended her complaint to include a challenge to that provision as well.

The prisons for which the positions had been advertised were all-male, maximum-security penitentiaries. The State authorities defended the restrictions on women employees, noting that inmates' living quarters were mostly dormitories, with communal showers and toilets.[6] Two of the facilities conducted outside employment schemes requiring routine strip searches of inmates upon re-entry.[7] In addition, "because of inadequate staff and facilities, no attempt [was] made ... to segregate inmates according to their offense or level of dangerousness." Accordingly, in defense of the exclusion of women employees in contact positions, it was argued that "[a] woman's relative ability to maintain order ... could be directly reduced by her womanhood."[8] The Court accepted those arguments, noting,

> There is a basis in fact for expecting that sex offenders who have criminally assaulted women in the past would be moved to do so again if access to women were established within the prison. There would also be a real risk that other inmates, deprived of a normal heterosexual environment, would assault women guards because they were women. In a prison system where violence is the order of the day, where inmate access to guards is facilitated by dormitory living arrangements, where every institution is under-staffed, and where a substantial portion of the inmate population is composed of sex offenders mixed at random with other prisoners, there are few visible deterrents to inmate assaults on women custodians.[9]

2.2   Factual and Normative Assertions

We will say that arguments in discrimination disputes include *factual* as well as *normative* components. The concept of *factual* assertions will be purely formal. It will assume nothing about the substantive truth of what is said. That is, it will assume nothing about what really happened in a given case, or about whose version of events is the most credible. Rather, it will denote *any version of the events, related in factual form*, either by the parties themselves or by other witnesses, judges or reporters. For example, it might be reported that Rawlinson alleged events *x* and *y* to have happened; and that the State authorities agreed that *x*

---

[5] *Id.* at 325 n. 6.
[6] *Id.* at 326.
[7] *Id.*
[8] *Id.* at 335.
[9] *Id.*

happened, but alleged z instead of y. We could then record their disagreement on the facts as follows,

A: $x \cdot y$

Z: $x \cdot z$

In tandem with their factual assertions, the parties to a dispute also make *normative* assertions, reflecting their view of how the law should be interpreted. If Ms. Rawlinson argues that the Court should find m, and the State authorities think that the Court should find n, we can write,

A: m

Z: n

Combining the factual and normative assertions, the parties' respective positions could be recorded as,

A: $(x \cdot y) \cdot m$

Z: $(x \cdot z) \cdot n$

2.3   Notation

We will use the letter T to represent a claim of "equal treatment." For example, we will say that the claimant in *Dothard* makes the *normative* claim that she *should be treated equally* to male applicants [A: T].

She also makes a *factual* claim that she has been treated *un*equally vis-à-vis male applicants. What kind of symbol might we then use to represent the assertion that treatment is *un*equal? The advantage of symbols is that we are free to choose any one we like. We could, for example, use the letter U, hence A: U. However, the economy of symbolic notation lies in its ability to display relationships among its components. The relationship between an assertion of equal treatment and an assertion of unequal treatment is a relationship of *mutual exclusion*. Certainly, where different kinds of treatment are at issue, a party might assert that some of the treatment is equal, and some, unequal; or that a given form of treatment was equal sometimes, and unequal at other times. However, as to any specific form of treatment at any specific time, a party making a factual assertion cannot, without self-contradiction, assert that the treatment is both equal and unequal. And a party making a normative assertion cannot, without self-contradiction, assert that a given treatment *ought to be* both equal *and* unequal.

Thus rather than introducing a new letter, we will use the symbol ~T to represent an assertion of "not equal treatment" or "unequal treatment." In her factual assertion, then, Ms. Rawlinson argues that she has been treated *unequally* to men [A: ~T]. On *that* point, the State authorities agree [Z: ~T]. They defend their action not by denying that the treatment is unequal, but by attempting to justify the factually unequal treatment on normative grounds. Of course, at this point, our notation form is still too crude. If we were merely to use the symbols T and ~T, it would be unclear whether the assertion in question is factual or normative. Therefore, in the following chapters, we will develop modified versions of these treatment symbols which will eliminate confusion.

But before completing this introduction to the two basic treatment symbols, let us add one more element. As the analysis progresses, it will sometimes be useful to speak about treatment generically, without specifying it as equal (T) or unequal (~T). In those cases, we will use the hierarchically superior symbol τ (tau). We will say that the symbols T and ~T represent hierarchically inferior values of the superior symbol τ. Accordingly, we will adopt our "first τ postulate,"

$$Ps(\tau_1) \quad \tau \subset T, \sim T$$

This is only our first τ postulate—hence the subscript numeral 1 (τ_1)—as a further postulate setting forth values for τ will appear later on. We will leave the *Dothard* case now for a little while, returning to it briefly in chapter 4, then again in chapter 6.

Exercise Set 2-1
Draw a tree diagram representing the values of τ.

Exercise Set 2-2
Translate (ignoring, for now, the distinction between factual and normative assertions).

Example: The claimant asserts that treatment should be equal.
Answer: A: T

1. The respondent conceded, without apology, that the treatment is unequal.
2. The respondent ardently believes that unequal treatment is legitimate in this case.
3. Some party has argued that the treatment is in fact equal.
4. It is the claimant who will argue that the treatment turned out to be equal.
5. The respondent made some argument about treatment.
6. Some party made some argument about treatment.

Answers to Exercises

Exercise Set 2-1

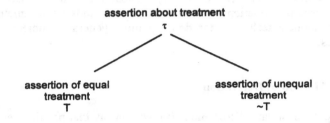

assertion about treatment
τ

assertion of equal
treatment
T

assertion of unequal
treatment
~T

Exercise Set 2-2

1. Z: ~T
4. A: T

2. Z: ~T
5. Z: τ

3. θ: T
6. θ: τ

3 Derivation of Arguments

We have seen that the values of symbols can be defined at various levels of generality, such that hierarchically superior ones (e.g., θ, τ) can represent hierarchically inferior ones (A, Z; T, ~T). Those hierarchical relationships will allow us to ascertain relationships among different kinds of arguments. In this chapter, we adopt a technique for deriving more general arguments from more specific ones.

3.1   The Method of Derivation

By applying the postulates $Ps(\theta)$ and $Ps(\tau)$, we can say that positions such as A: T, A: ~T, Z: T and Z: ~T all take the more general form θ: τ. As the relationships among those symbols are still very simple, that operation can be performed mentally. However, as we continue to add elements, greater numbers of mental steps will be required in order to derive general arguments from more specific ones. It will therefore be useful to have a technique for deriving arguments in written form. The technique will be as follows. To the left of each step, we will place a number in parentheses, to show which step it is. To the right of each step, we will indicate a justification for the step. As a first step, we will simply state as "given" the argument from which the derivation is proceeding. The final step will be the conclusion ($\therefore$). For example,

> *From* A: T *derive* θ: τ,
> (1)   A: T   argument given
> (2) θ: T $Ps(\theta)$
> $\therefore$ θ: τ $Ps(\tau_1)$

As postulates may be introduced in different orders, there will often be more than one way to derive an argument,

> *From* A: T *derive* θ: τ,
> (1)   A: T   argument given
> (2)   A: τ $Ps(\tau_1)$
> $\therefore$ θ: τ $Ps(\theta)$

As a result, the answers provided at the end of each chapter will often represent only one approach.

Exercise Set 3-1

1. *Derive* Z: τ *from* Z: ~T.
2. *Derive* θ: T *from* A: T.
3. *Derive* θ: τ *from* θ: ~T.
4. *Derive* θ: τ *from* Z: ~T.

3.2 Invalid Inference

In order to derive an argument, we may only move "up" the ladder of generality, substituting hierarchically superior symbols in the place of inferior ones, in order to ascertain a more general expression of the original argument. We may not move in the opposite direction, as that would entail fallacies. For example, the following derivation would be invalid, as it is inadmissible to derive a specific argument from a more general one,

From θ: τ *derive* A: T,
   (1)   θ: τ   argument given
   (2)   A: τ   Ps(θ)
   ∴   A: T   Ps(τ₁)

That demonstration contains two errors. In step (2), the value A is inferred from θ. That inference is invalid, however, since A is only one possible value of θ. Similarly, in the concluding step, the value T is erroneously inferred from τ, as T represents only one possible value of τ. While it is necessarily the case that θ: τ derives from A: T, it is not necessarily the case that A: T derives from θ: τ. That is because θ: τ can also yield the arguments Z: T, A: ~T, or Z: ~T. We will limit the derivations of arguments to those arguments which necessarily derive from other arguments. In order to see more clearly the kind of error which could result if we were to allow steps moving "down" the ladder of generality, consider the following derivation,

From A: T *derive* Z: T,
   (1)   A: T   argument given
   (2)   θ: T   Ps(θ)
   ∴   Z: T   Ps(θ)

It is true that A and Z *might* agree that treatment is, or should be, equal, but it hardly follows as a matter of course. In deriving arguments, we will never allow a step which represents a mere possibility. We will limit ourselves only to steps which necessarily follow from prior steps.

Exercise Set 3-2

Mark the following derivations as either valid or invalid.

1. θ: T *derives from* Z: T.
2. Z: T *derives from* θ: T.
3. Z: ~T *derives from* A: ~T.
4. A: τ *derives from* A: ~T.
5. θ: τ *derives from* A: ~T.
6. A: τ *derives from* θ: τ.

Answers to Exercises

Exercise Set 3-1

1. (1) Z: ~T   argument given
    ∴   Z: τ   Ps(τ₁)

3. (1) θ: ~T   argument given
    ∴   θ: τ   Ps(τ₁)

2. (1) A: T   argument given
    ∴   θ: T   Ps(θ)

4. (1) Z: ~T   argument given
    (2) θ: ~T   Ps(θ)
    ∴   θ: τ   Ps(τ₁)

Exercise Set 3-2

1. valid   2. invalid   3. invalid
4. valid   5. valid   6. invalid

4 Normative Positions

In chapters 2 and 3, we suspended the distinction between factual and normative assertions in order to focus on the basic difference between assertions of equal and unequal treatment. In this chapter, concepts from deontic logic are introduced as means of designating certain assertions as normative.

4.1 Deontic Concepts

Formal logic divides into various areas. One of them is *deontic* logic, the logic of norms.[1] Deontic logic sets forth relationships linking such concepts as "obligation," "prohibition" and "permission." We will not require detailed study of deontic logic, as we will use only some basic concepts.[2]

The concepts of *obligation* and *permission* will be of particular interest when we turn to arguments of a normative character. The relationships which can be drawn between these concepts will recall the kinds of relationships set forth by Hohfeld, but we will not examine that matter further here.[3] For now, suffice it to say that we will examine certain kinds of statements in which a party argues that the law *requires* a given result. They will be called *compulsory assertions*. We will denote them by attaching the *marker*—that is, a superscript letter—"c" to some value of τ. For example, since T represents the assertion "Treatment *is* equal," T^c will represent the assertion "It is compulsory that treatment be equal" or "The law requires equal treatment."[4] Compulsory assertions will be distinguished from *permissive* assertions, which we will represent with the superscript letter "p". Thus T^p would signify the assertion "It is permissible for treatment to be equal" or "The law permits equal treatment in this case." Assume, then, the following values for T and ~T,

T = "Treatment is equal"   ~T = "Treatment is unequal"

---

[1] The word comes from the Greek *deon*, meaning "obligation." See Introduction, note 21 *supra*.

[2] Cf. the use of deontic analysis in Heinze, 2003b.

[3] Cf. Heinze 2003a: Introduction.

[4] While the placement of deontic components in superscript position departs from dominant usage, it will be adopted in this study in order to maintain a primary focus on the τ symbols to which it is attached. For an overview of more customary notation forms in deontic logic, see, e.g., Kalinowski, 1972.

For those values, we can adopt the following deontic concepts.[5] As the analysis progresses, we will see that all of them do in fact appear in non-discrimination jurisprudence,

T^c = "It is compulsory that treatment be equal" or "The law requires equal treatment "

$\sim T^c$ = "It is compulsory that treatment be unequal" or "The law requires unequal treatment "

T^p = "It is permissible that treatment be equal" or "The law permits equal treatment "

$\sim T^p$ = "It is permissible that treatment be unequal" or "The law permits unequal treatment "

T^{-c} = "It is not compulsory that treatment be equal" or "The law does not require equal treatment "

$\sim T^{-c}$ = "It is not compulsory that treatment be unequal" or "The law does not require unequal treatment "

T^{-p} = "It is not permissible for treatment to be equal" or "The law does not permit equal treatment "

$\sim T^{-p}$ = "It is not permissible that treatment be unequal" or "The law does not permit unequal treatment "

We will also adopt some *formulas* (F.) which set forth relationships among these concepts. Note the following *relationships of equivalence* between the concepts of compulsory and permissive norms,[6]

F.4-1 $\quad T^c = \sim T^{-p}$ $\qquad$ F.4-2 $\quad T^p = \sim T^{-c}$
F.4-3 $\quad T^{-c} = \sim T^{p}$ $\qquad$ F.4-4 $\quad T^{-p} = \sim T^{c}$

These formulas show that any compulsory assertion can be expressed in terms of a permissive assertion, and any permissive assertion can be expressed in terms of a compulsory assertion.

4.2   Normative Treatment Postulates

Recall that the first τ postulate includes only elements of equal and non-equal treatment,

$\mathrm{Ps}(\tau_1) \quad \tau \subset T, \sim T$

---

[5] Note that the concept of a *prohibition* could be fit into the framework as an alternative way of asserting that something is *not permissible* (~p).

[6] Cf. Section 1.6, note 8 *supra*. Again, a biconditional representation is arguably more prudent, but, within the framework of the model, we will stipulate that these relationships of equivalence establish identity between each pair of terms.

It provides no information about the factual or normative character of an assertion. We can now adopt postulates to reflect values for τ in normative assertions,

$$Ps(\tau^c) \quad \tau^c \subset T^c, \sim T^c$$

$$Ps(\tau^p) \quad \tau^p \subset T^p, \sim T^p$$

For *Dothard*, the parties' normative positions can now be written to reflect more accurately their disagreement. The claimant's normative position can be written A: T^c, and the respondent's normative position as Z: $\sim T^p$.

Exercise Set 4-1

Translate.

Example: The claimant asserts that equal treatment is required.
Answer: A: T^c

1. The respondent replies that equal treatment is not required.
2. The respondent replies that unequal treatment is permitted.
3. The claimant insists that unequal treatment is not required.
4. Some party replies that unequal treatment is permitted.
5. Some party makes some permissive assertion about treatment.
6. The claimant responds with a compulsory assertion about treatment.
7. The claimant replies that unequal treatment is not prohibited.

Exercise Set 4-2

Rewrite the following positions in terms of permissive and non-permissive assertions.

Example: A: T^c
Answer: A: $\sim T^{\sim p}$

1. Z: $T^{\sim c}$
2. θ: $\sim T^c$
3. Z: $\sim T^{\sim c}$
4. A: $\sim\sim T^c$
5. θ: $\sim T^{\sim c}$
6. θ: $\sim\sim\sim T^{\sim c}$
7. A: $T^c \cdot T^{\sim p}$
8. A: $T^c \rightarrow \sim T^{\sim c}$
9. θ: $T^c \cdot \sim T^{\sim c}$
10. Z: $\sim T^{\sim c} \cdot \sim\sim\sim T^p$

Exercise Set 4-3

Rewrite the following positions in terms of compulsory and non-compulsory assertions.

Example: A: T^p
Answer: A: $\sim T^{\sim c}$

  1. θ: $\sim T^p$ 2.   Z: $\sim\sim T^p$
  3.   Z: $\sim T^{\sim p}$ 4. θ: $\sim\sim T^{\sim p} \rightarrow T^{\sim c}$
  5. θ: $T^p \rightarrow \sim T^p$ 6. θ: $\sim\sim T^{\sim p} \cdot \sim\sim\sim T^{\sim\sim c}$
  7.   A: $\sim\sim T^{\sim\sim p} \rightarrow \sim T^{\sim\sim\sim c}$

Exercise Set 4-4

Provide alternative notation forms for problems 1 – 4 in Exercise Set 4-1.

Example: The claimant asserts that equal treatment is required.
Answer: A: $\sim T^{\sim p}$

4.3   Non-Contradiction

We have adopted from classical logic the assumption that for a given proposition X, it cannot be the case that X and ~X are both true.[7] We will accept that a party might adopt two conflicting positions in order to adduce distinct arguments, e.g., in order to argue in the alternative, but not to express any one argument. We will therefore assume that no party asserts, as part of the *same* argument, that the law *requires* equal treatment *and* that the law *does not require* equal treatment,

F.4-5 $\sim(T^c \cdot T^{\sim c})$ *"It is not the case that the law requires equal treatment and that it does not require equal treatment."*

---

[7] This principle is commonly known as the "law of contradiction" (or the "law of non-contradiction"). Detlefsen *et al.*, 1999: 60. It is related to the concept of negation adopted in Section 1.6, text accompanying note 7 *supra*.

Similarly, we will assume that no party asserts, as part of the same argument, that the law *requires* unequal treatment *and* that the law *does not require* unequal treatment,

F.4-6 $\sim(\sim T^c \cdot \sim T^{\sim c})$ *"It is not the case that the law requires unequal treatment **and** that it does not require unequal treatment."*

Hence, for *any* argument τ about treatment,

F.4-7 $\sim(\tau^c \cdot \tau^{\sim c})$ *"It is not the case that the law requires a given treatment **and** that it does not require that treatment."*

Note that the relationships of equivalence in F.4-1 to F.4-4 allow alternative formulations of these principles. For example, applying F.4-3 to F.4-5, we can say,

F.4-8 $\sim(T^c \cdot \sim T^p)$ *"It is not the case that the law requires equal treatment **and** that it permits unequal treatment."*

In the same way, we will assume that no party asserts, as part of the same argument, that the law *permits* equal treatment *and* that the law *does not permit* equal treatment,

F.4-9 $\sim(T^p \cdot T^{\sim p})$ *"It is not the case that the law permits equal treatment **and** that it prohibits (does not permit) equal treatment."*

Similarly, we will assume that no party asserts, as part of the same argument, that the law *permits* unequal treatment *and* that the law *does not permit* unequal treatment,

F.4-10 $\sim(\sim T^p \cdot \sim T^{\sim p})$ *"It is not the case that the law permits unequal treatment **and** that it prohibits unequal treatment."*

Hence, for *any* argument τ about treatment,

F.4-11 $\sim(\tau^p \cdot \tau^{\sim p})$ *"It is not the case that the law permits a given treatment **and** that it prohibits that treatment."*

By extension, we will accept as an intuitive matter,

F.4-5'	$\sim(T^c \rightarrow T^{\sim c})$	F.4-6'	$\sim(\sim T^c \rightarrow \sim T^{\sim c})$
F.4-5"	$\sim(T^{\sim c} \rightarrow T^c)$	F.4-6"	$\sim(\sim T^{\sim c} \rightarrow \sim T^c)$
F.4-9'	$\sim(T^p \rightarrow T^{\sim p})$	F.4-10'	$\sim(\sim T^p \rightarrow \sim T^{\sim p})$
F.4-9"	$\sim(T^{\sim p} \rightarrow T^p)$	F.4-10"	$\sim(\sim T^{\sim p} \rightarrow \sim T^p)$

4.4   Necessary Conditional Relationships

Note the following *necessary conditional relationships*, which we will accept as axiomatic, i.e., as true by definition. First, something can be compulsory only if it is permitted. For example, if the law *requires* that I pay income tax—and assuming no conflicting norm[8]—then it by definition *permits* me to do so. Similarly, if equal treatment is compulsory, then, necessarily, it is permitted,

F.4-12 $T^c \rightarrow T^p$

And if *un*equal treatment is compulsory, then, necessarily, it is permitted,

F.4-13 $\sim T^c \rightarrow \sim T^p$

Thus, *for any argument* τ *about treatment, if that treatment is compulsory, then it is permitted,*

F.4-14 $\tau^c \rightarrow \tau^p$

In addition, if something is prohibited, then, necessarily, it is not compulsory: if I am not permitted to shoplift, then by definition I am not required to shoplift. Thus if equal treatment prohibited, then, necessarily, it is not compulsory,

F.4-15 $T^{\sim p} \rightarrow T^{\sim c}$

And if *un*equal treatment is *not* permitted, then, necessarily, it is not compulsory,

F.4-16 $\sim T^{\sim p} \rightarrow \sim T^{\sim c}$

Thus, *for any argument* τ *about treatment, if that treatment is prohibited, then it is not compulsory,*

F.4-17 $\tau^{\sim p} \rightarrow \tau^{\sim c}$

---

[8] The possibility of conflicting norms, e.g., in multi-jurisdictional contexts suggests limitations on the applicability of deontic concepts. See, e.g., Rodes and Pospesel, 1997: 336 note 3, and 345-46. In this study, however, our concern is not with the correct resolution of disputes, but only with the construction of arguments on either side of a dispute, insofar as the very task of either party is to adduce positions which (purport to) resolve any such inconsistencies.

4.5   Tautologies

The logical concept of "tautology" is not as simple as one might think. Without examining it in detail here, we will accept as axiomatic that any proposition implies itself. That is, for any proposition p, it is the case that $p \rightarrow p$. We can therefore accept as axiomatic,

F.4-18	$T^c \rightarrow T^c$	F.4-19	$T^p \rightarrow T^p$
F.4-20	$\sim T^c \rightarrow \sim T^c$	F.4-21	$\sim T^p \rightarrow \sim T^p$
F.4-22	$T^{-c} \rightarrow T^{-c}$	F.4-23	$T^{-p} \rightarrow T^{-p}$
F.4-24	$\sim T^{-c} \rightarrow \sim T^{-c}$	F.4-25	$\sim T^{-p} \rightarrow \sim T^{-p}$

4.6   Fallacies

Under F.4-12, the position A: T^c necessarily implies A: T^p. Under F.4-18, it also implies itself. We can therefore say that A: T^c implies A: $T^c \cdot T^p$. Similarly, under F.4-15, θ: T^{-p} necessarily implies θ: T^{-c}, and thus, under F.4-23 also implies θ: $T^{-p} \cdot T^{-c}$. By contrast, the following relationship, although possibly true under some circumstances, is not necessarily true,

F.4-26 $T^p \rightarrow T^c$

For example, the fact that I am permitted to purchase a legally vended newspaper does not imply that I am required to purchase it. It would be erroneous to adopt the proposition $T^p \rightarrow T^c$ as axiomatic, as there are circumstances in which it would be false.

In casual speech, we might sometimes construe the assertion that something is permitted to imply that it *is not* compulsory. For example, we ordinarily think that the fact that I am permitted to purchase a newspaper implies that I am *not* required to purchase it. Similarly, we might surmise that, if a given form of equal treatment is designated as being permissible, it is therefore not compulsory,

F.4-27 $T^p \rightarrow T^{-c}$

However, that proposition too, albeit true in some cases, will not be true in all cases, and cannot be accepted as axiomatic. Under F.4-12, the very reason why something (e.g., equal treatment) is permitted *may* be that is required ($T^c \rightarrow T^p$). Under those circumstances, it would be contradictory to say that T, being permissible, is *not* compulsory.[9] (By analogy, the fact that I am permitted to pay

---

[9] The contradiction can be displayed by means of the rule of hypothetical syllogism, which follows the general form,

taxes does not necessarily imply that I am not required to do so: in most cases, the reason I am permitted to do so is that I am required to do so.)

Similarly, the fact that I am not required to purchase the newspaper does not imply that I am not permitted to do so. By extension, assuming that equal treatment is not compulsory, it does not follow that it is prohibited. The following relationship might hold in some situations, but cannot be accepted as axiomatic,

F.4-28 $T^{-c} \to T^{-p}$

Alternatively, in casual speech, we might sometimes construe the assertion that something is not compulsory (like purchasing a newspaper) to imply that it *is* permitted,

F.4-29 $T^{-c} \to T^{p}$

---

(1) $p \to q$
(2) $q \to r$
$\therefore$ $p \to r$

That is, if the propositions $p \to q$ and $q \to r$ are true, then the proposition $p \to r$ must necessarily be true. For example, given the following values of p, q and r,

p = Socrates is a philosopher.
q = Socrates is a human being.
r = Socrates descends from apes.

We can then reason as follows,

If Socrates is a philosopher, then Socrates is a human being.
If Socrates is a human being, then Socrates descends from apes.
Therefore, if Socrates is a philosopher, then Socrates descends from apes.

We will accept that premises may appear in any order. Hence, it would be equally valid to say,

(1) $q \to r$
(2) $p \to q$
$\therefore$ $p \to r$

Hence,

(1) $T^{p} \to T^{-c}$ We shall test step (1) to determine whether it can entail a fallacy.
(2) $T^{c} \to T^{p}$ Step (2) is axiomatic under F.4-12, and therefore cannot be fallacious.
$\therefore$ $T^{c} \to T^{-c}$ This step contradicts F.4-5'. If step (2) cannot be fallacious, then step 1 is fallacious.

Once again, such an assertion holds only under certain circumstances, and not under all circumstances. Under F.4-15, the very reason why equal treatment is not compulsory *may* be that is *not* permissible ($T^{-p} \rightarrow T^{-c}$). Under those circumstances, it would be contradictory to say that T, not being compulsory, is permissible.[10] (By analogy, the fact that I am not required to litter does not mean that I am permitted to do so: presumably, the reason I am not required to litter is that I am *not permitted* to litter.)

Exercise Set 4-5

Which of the following formulas is necessarily true?

1. $\sim T^c \rightarrow \sim T^c$ 2. $\sim T^c \rightarrow T^{-p}$
3. $T^p \rightarrow \sim T^p$ 4. $T^{-c} \rightarrow T^p$
5. $T^{-c} \rightarrow \sim T^p$ 6. $\sim T^{-p} \rightarrow T^p$
7. $T^{-p} \rightarrow \sim T^c$ 8. $T^p \rightarrow T^{-c}$
9. $\sim(T^c \cdot T^{-c})$ 10. $\tau^{-p} \rightarrow \tau^{-c}$

4.7 The Unspecified Marker

It will at times be useful to designate an assertion as normative, without indicating whether it is compulsory or permissive. In particular, we may wish to distinguish normative assertions from factual assertions, without further designating the normative assertions as compulsory or permissive. The superscript letter γ (gamma) marker will be used to serve that purpose (τ^γ),

     $Ps(\gamma)$ $\gamma \subset c, p$

     $Ps(\tau^\gamma)$ $\tau^\gamma \subset \tau^c, \tau^p$

The symbol τ^γ thus represents any normative assertion about treatment, compulsory or permissive. Accordingly, to say that some party makes some normative assertion, we would write $\theta: \tau^\gamma$ (see Figure 4-1).

---

[10] As in note 9 *supra*, the contradiction arises as follows,

     (1) $T^{-c} \rightarrow T^p$ We shall test step (1) to determine whether it can entail a fallacy.
     (2) $T^{-p} \rightarrow T^{-c}$ Step (2) is axiomatic under F.4-15, and therefore cannot be fallacious.
     $\therefore$ $T^{-p} \rightarrow T^p$ This step contradicts F.4-9". If step (2) cannot be fallacious, then step 1 is fallacious.

4.8   Deriving Arguments

Relationships of equivalence and necessary conditional relationships can be introduced as steps in proofs in order to derive arguments. As a justifying step, a relationship of equivalence can be marked "RE", and a necessary conditional relationship can be marked "NCR". For example,

From A: T^c *derive* θ: $\sim T^{\sim p}$

(1)	A: T^c	argument given
(2)	θ: T^c	Ps(θ)
∴	θ: $\sim T^{\sim p}$	RE

From A: T^c *derive* θ: T^p

(1)	A: T^c	argument given
(2)	θ: T^c	Ps(θ)
∴	θ: T^p	NCR

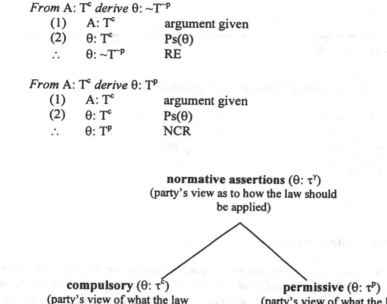

normative assertions $(\theta: \tau^\gamma)$
(party's view as to how the law should be applied)

compulsory $(\theta: \tau^c)$
(party's view of what the law requires)

permissive $(\theta: \tau^p)$
(party's view of what the law permits)

"Equal treatment is required" $(\theta: T^c)$

"Unequal treatment is required" $(\theta: \sim T^c)$

"Equal treatment is permitted" $(\theta: T^p)$

"Unequal treatment is permitted" $(\theta: \sim T^p)$

Figure 4-1

Exercise Set 4-6

1. *Derive Z: τ^c from Z: $\sim T^c$.*
3. *Derive θ: τ^c from Z: $T^{\sim p}$.*
5. *Derive θ: τ^p from Z: $\sim T^c$.*
7. *Derive θ: τ^γ from Z: $\sim T^c$.*

2. *Derive θ: τ^p from A: T^p.*
4. *Derive θ: τ^p from A: $\sim T^{\sim c}$.*
6. *Derive A: τ^γ from A: T^c.*
8. *Derive θ: τ^γ from A: $\sim T^{\sim p}$.*

Answers to Exercises

Exercise Set 4-1

1. Z: $T^{\sim c}$
3. A: $\sim T^{\sim c}$
5. θ: τ^p
7. A: $\sim T^p$ (A: $\sim T^{\sim p}$)

2. Z: $\sim T^p$
4. θ: $\sim T^p$
6. A: τ^c

Exercise Set 4-2

1. Z: $\sim T^p$
3. Z: $T^{\sim p}$
5. θ: T^p
7. A: $\sim T^{\sim p} \cdot T^p$
9. θ: $\sim T^{\sim p} \cdot T^p$

2. θ: $T^{\sim p}$
4. A: $\sim T^{\sim p}$
6. θ: T^p
8. A: $\sim T^{\sim p} \to T^p$
10. Z: $T^{\sim p} \cdot \sim T^p$

1. θ: $T^{\sim c}$
3. Z: $T^{\sim c}$
5. θ: $\sim T^c \to T^{\sim c}$
7. A: $\sim T^{\sim c} \to \sim T^c$

2. Z: $\sim T^c$
4. θ: $\sim T^c \to T^{\sim c}$
6. θ: $\sim T^c \cdot \sim T^c$

Exercise Set 4-4

1. Z: ~T^p
3. A: T^p

2. Z: T^{-c}
4. θ: T^{-c}

Exercise Set 4-5

The formulas in problems 1, 2, 5, 6, 7, 9 and 10 are necessarily true.

Exercise Set 4-6

1. (1) Z: ~T^c given
    ∴   Z: τ^c Ps(τ^c)

2. (1) A: T^p given
    (2) θ: T^p Ps(θ)
    ∴   θ: τ^p Ps(τ^p)

3. (1) Z: T^{-p} given
    (2) θ: T^{-p} Ps(θ)
    (3) θ: ~T^c RE
    ∴   θ: τ^c Ps(τ^c)

4. (1) A: ~T^{-c} given
    (2) θ: ~T^{-c} Ps(θ)
    (3) θ: T^p RE
    ∴   θ: τ^p Ps(τ^p)

5. (1) Z: ~T^c given
    (2) θ: ~T^c Ps(θ)
    (3) θ: ~T^p NCR
    ∴   θ: τ^p Ps(τ^p)

6. (1) A: T^c given
    (2) A: τ^c Ps(τ^c)
    ∴   A: τ^γ Ps(τ^γ)

7. (1) Z: ~T^c given
    (2) θ: ~T^c Ps(θ)
    (3) θ: τ^c Ps(τ^c)
    ∴   θ: τ^γ Ps(τ^γ)

8. (1) A: ~T^{-p} given
    (2) θ: ~T^{-p} Ps(θ)
    (3) θ: T^c RE
    (4) θ: τ^c Ps(τ^c)
    ∴   θ: τ^γ Ps(τ^γ)

5 Theorems

We have examined a number of postulates, which state relationships between symbols at different hierarchical levels. In this chapter we adopt a method, similar to that for deriving arguments, of generating more economical ways of stating values for certain higher-order symbols.

5.1 Theorems

By combining postulates, we can generate more precise, definitions for hierarchically superior symbols. The term *theorem* will be used to denote a formula that derives a set of values of a symbol from one or more postulates. For example, by combining $Ps(\tau^\gamma)$ and $Ps(\tau^c)$, we can obtain a more precise value for τ^γ. Hence one possible theorem which would provide an alternative definition of τ^γ,

$$\tau^\gamma \subset T^c, \sim T^c, \tau^p$$

As the analysis progresses, it will be helpful to have a technique for proving theorems—deriving them from postulates—in recorded form. We will do so by a technique of progressive steps, similar to the method of deriving arguments. Note that the first step is not merely justified as "given," but rather states some starting postulate. For example,

> *Prove the theorem:* $\tau^\gamma \subset T^c, \sim T^c, \tau^p$
> (1) $\tau^\gamma \subset \tau^c, \tau^p$ $Ps(\tau^\gamma)$
> ∴ $\tau^\gamma \subset T^c, \sim T^c, \tau^p$ $Ps(\tau^c)$

The same result can be achieved regardless of the order in which the postulates are introduced,

> *Prove the theorem:* $\tau^\gamma \subset T^c, \sim T^c, \tau^p$
> (1) $\tau^c \subset T^c, \sim T^c$ $Ps(\tau^c)$
> ∴ $\tau^\gamma \subset T^c, \sim T^c, \tau^p$ $Ps(\tau^\gamma)$

As with the derivation of arguments, answers provided for exercise sets will, in some cases, represent only one possible approach.

39

Exercise Set 5-1

Derive the following theorems.

1. $\tau^\gamma \subset \tau^c$, T^p, $\sim T^p$
2. $\tau^\gamma \subset T^c$, $\sim T^c$, T^p, $\sim T^p$
3. $\tau^\gamma \subset T^c$, $\sim T^c$, $\sim T^{\sim c}$, $T^{\sim c}$
4. $\tau^\gamma \subset \sim T^{\sim p}$, $T^{\sim p}$, T^p, $\sim T^p$

Even a small number of postulates can generate a considerable number of theorems. For example, Exercise Set 5-1 sets forth four different theorems that state values for the symbol τ^γ. However, not all theorems are equally useful. The theorem in problem 2 is helpful insofar as it displays all of the most specific values of τ^γ precisely as they appear in Figure 4.1. By contrast, the theorem in problems 1, 3 and 4 provides only some practice in using postulates, and will not be important as a general matter. Accordingly, the Appendix will provide a record of all postulates, but only of the more significant theorems,

$$\text{Th}(\tau^\gamma) \quad \tau^\gamma \subset T^c, \sim T^c, T^p, \sim T^p$$

Theorems can be used just like postulates to justify steps taken in deriving arguments or proving other theorems. In order to keep the steps predictable, we will use *only theorems appearing in the Appendix* when writing proofs. Moreover, as with postulates, theorems can sometimes be introduced in different orders, thus allowing for more than one correct answer.

5.2   Valid and Invalid Inference

The process of proving theorems moves in the opposite direction from the process of deriving arguments. To derive an argument, we must move 'up' the ladder of generality, substituting hierarchically inferior symbols for superior ones, in order to ascertain a more general statement of the original argument. To prove a theorem, we must move 'down' the ladder of generality in order to ascertain a set of more specific values of a symbol. For example, it is permissible to move down the ladder by saying that any value of τ^c represents a value of τ^γ. However, we cannot move up the ladder by allowing τ^γ to represent any given value of τ^c. That is, from the postulate $\tau^\gamma \subset \tau^c$, τ^p we cannot adopt the theorem $\tau^c \subset \tau^\gamma$ or the theorem $\tau^p \subset \tau^\gamma$. Thus, in the following proof, both steps are fallacious,

> *Prove the theorem:* $T^c \subset \tau^\gamma$
> (1) $T^c \subset \tau^c$ $\text{Ps}(\tau^c)$
> $\therefore$ $T^c \subset \tau^\gamma$ $\text{Ps}(\tau^\gamma)$

Answers to Exercises

Exercise Set 5-1

1.   (1) $\tau^\gamma \subset \tau^c, \tau^p$ $Ps(\tau^\gamma)$
    $\therefore$ $\tau^\gamma \subset \tau^c, T^p, {\sim}T^p$ $Ps(\tau^p)$

2.   (1) $\tau^\gamma \subset \tau^c, \tau^p$ $Ps(\tau^\gamma)$
    (2) $\tau^\gamma \subset T^c, {\sim}T^c, \tau^p$ $Ps(\tau^c)$
    $\therefore$ $\tau^\gamma \subset T^c, {\sim}T^c, T^p, {\sim}T^p$ $Ps(\tau^p)$

3.   (1) $\tau^\gamma \subset \tau^c, \tau^p$ $Ps(\tau^\gamma)$
    (2) $\tau^\gamma \subset T^c, {\sim}T^c, \tau^p$ $Ps(\tau^c)$
    (3) $\tau^\gamma \subset T^c, {\sim}T^c, T^p, {\sim}T^p$ $Ps(\tau^p)$
    (4) $\tau^\gamma \subset T^c, {\sim}T^c, {\sim}T^c, {\sim}T^p$ RE
    $\therefore$ $\tau^\gamma \subset T^c, {\sim}T^c, {\sim}T^c, T^c$ RE

4.   (1) $\tau^\gamma \subset \tau^c, \tau^p$ $Ps(\tau^\gamma)$
    (2) $\tau^\gamma \subset T^c, {\sim}T^c, \tau^p$ $Ps(\tau^c)$
    (3) $\tau^\gamma \subset T^c, {\sim}T^c, T^p, {\sim}T^p$ $Ps(\tau^p)$
    (4) $\tau^\gamma \subset {\sim}T^p, {\sim}T^c, T^p, {\sim}T^p$ RE
    $\therefore$ $\tau^\gamma \subset {\sim}T^p, T^p, T^p, {\sim}T^p$ RE

6   General Schema of Assertions

Having developed a notation for normative assertions about treatment, we can now adopt a more precise form for factual assertions.

6.1   Notation

We have seen that normative assertions can be expressed in compulsory or permissive terms. By contrast, factual assumptions do not, for our purposes, break down into particular kinds. Their only distinguishing feature is that they are *not normative*. Accordingly, the marker $\sim\!\gamma$ will be used to denote *factual* (i.e., non-normative) assertions about treatment.

That choice of marker is not obvious. As a general matter, the fact that an utterance is not normative does not necessarily make it factual. It could be some other kind of utterance, like a question or an exclamation. However, for purposes of our model, we are excluding any other kind of utterance. We are admitting only factual and normative utterances, such that any utterance that is not normative is factual, and any utterance that is not factual is normative. We are constructing a relationship of mutual exclusion between normative and factual assertions: we will not recognize any assertions about treatment except insofar as we can designate them as being either formally normative (γ) or formally factual ($\sim\!\gamma$).

Again, by describing an assertion as formally "factual," we assume nothing about its substantive truth. That characterization will mean only that the assertion is expressed in factual, as opposed to normative, language. For example, the assertion "women and men are treated unequally" is formally factual regardless of whether it is substantively true (indeed, regardless of whether it is unequivocally meaningful), and regardless of the kind of evidence that is introduced to support it. In *Dothard*, the claimant asserts that treatment of men and women is in fact unequal [A: $\sim\!T^{\sim\gamma}$] and the State authorities concede that argument [Z: $\sim\!T^{\sim\gamma}$]. Their disagreement is normative, not factual.

As with normative assertions, it will also at times be useful to denote a factual assertion, without specifying whether it is an assertion of equal treatment or of unequal treatment. For that purpose, we will use the symbol $\tau^{\sim\gamma}$. Hence,

$$Ps(\tau^{\sim\gamma}) \qquad \tau^{\sim\gamma} \subset T^{\sim\gamma}, \sim\!T^{\sim\gamma}$$

If we wished to say that some party makes some factual assertion about treatment, without specifying whether that assertion is an assertion of equal treatment [θ: T⁻ᵞ] or unequal treatment [θ: ~T⁻ᵞ], we would use the more general formula θ: τ⁻ᵞ.

Exercise Set 6-1

Translate.

Example: The claimant asserts that treatment is unequal.
Answer: A: ~T⁻ᵞ

1. The respondent corporation conceded that the treatment was unequal.
2. Some party claimed that the treatment was equal.
3. The respondent explained why unequal treatment was justified.
4. The claimant made some factual assertion about treatment.
5. Someone clearly made some factual argument about treatment.
6. The respondent retorts angrily with an assertion about treatment.
7. Some party makes some assertion about treatment.

Exercise Set 6-2

1. *Derive* A: τ⁻ᵞ *from* A: ~T⁻ᵞ.
2. *Derive* θ: τ⁻ᵞ *from* Z: ~T⁻ᵞ

6.2   General Schema of Assertions about Treatment

We have divided all assertions about treatment into normative assertions and factual assertions. The unmarked τ can be used to designate all possible assertions about treatment, be they normative or factual. Hence a second postulate setting forth values of τ (compare it with Ps(τ₁)),

$$Ps(τ_2) \quad τ \subset τ^{ᵞ}, τ^{⁻ᵞ}$$

Exercise Set 6-3

Derive these theorems using only postulates.

1. $\tau \subset \tau^c, \tau^p, \tau^{\gamma}$
2. $\tau \subset T^c, \sim T^c, T^p, \sim T^p, T^{\gamma}, \sim T^{\gamma}$

Now recall the observation made in the last chapter, that theorems of particular interest would be recorded in the Appendix, and could be introduced into proofs as a means of performing them in fewer steps.

Exercise Set 6-4

Redo Exercise Set 6-2, problem 2, using the fewest possible steps.

In Exercise Set 6-3 and Exercise Set 6-4, the theorem proved in problem 2 is of interest, as it states all of the most specific values of τ. It is therefore included in the Appendix,

$$\text{Th}(\tau) \quad \tau \subset T^c, \sim T^c, T^p, \sim T^p, T^{\gamma}, \sim T^{\gamma}$$

Exercise Set 6-5

1. *Draw a tree diagram to represent the relationships among the symbols τ^{γ}, T^{γ} and $\sim T^{\gamma}$.*

2. *Draw a tree diagram representing all values of τ.*

Answers to Exercises

Exercise Set 6-1

1. Z: $\sim$T$^{\gamma}$
2. θ: T$^{\gamma}$
3. Z: $\sim$T^{p}
4. A: τ^{γ}

5. θ: τ^{γ}
6. Z: τ
7. θ: τ

Exercise Set 6-2

1. (1)   A: $\sim$T$^{\gamma}$ given
    $\therefore$ A: $\tau^{\sim\gamma}$ Ps($\tau^{\sim\gamma}$)

2. (1)   Z: $\sim$T$^{\gamma}$ given
    (2) θ: $\sim$T$^{\gamma}$ Ps(θ)
    $\therefore$ θ: $\tau^{\sim\gamma}$ Ps($\tau^{\sim\gamma}$)

Exercise Set 6-3

1. (1) $\tau \subset \tau^{\gamma}, \tau^{\gamma}$ Ps(τ_2)
    $\therefore$ $\tau \subset \tau^c, \tau^p, \tau^{\gamma}$ Ps(τ^{γ})

2. (1) $\tau \subset \tau^{\gamma}, \tau^{\gamma}$ Ps(τ_2)
    (2) $\tau \subset \tau^c, \tau^p, \tau^{\gamma}$ Ps(τ^{γ})
    (3) $\tau \subset$ T^c, $\sim$T^c, τ^p, τ^{γ} Ps(τ^c)
    (4) $\tau \subset$ T^c, $\sim$T^c, T^p, $\sim$T^p, τ^{γ} Ps(τ^p)
    $\therefore$ $\tau \subset$ T^c, $\sim$T^c, T^p, $\sim$T^p,   Ps(τ^{γ})
                T$^{\gamma}$, $\sim$T$^{\gamma}$

Exercise Set 6-4

(1) $\tau \subset \tau^{\gamma}, \tau^{\gamma}$ Ps(τ_2)
(2) $\tau \subset$ T^c, $\sim$T^c, T^p, $\sim$T^p, τ^{γ} Th(τ^{γ})
$\therefore$ $\tau \subset$ T^c, $\sim$T^c, T^p, $\sim$T^p, T$^{\gamma}$, $\sim$T$^{\gamma}$ Ps(τ^p)

Exercise Set 6-5

1.

τ^{γ}
(factual assertion about treatment)

T$^{\gamma}$
"Treatment is equal"

$\sim$T$^{\gamma}$
"Treatment is unequal"

2.

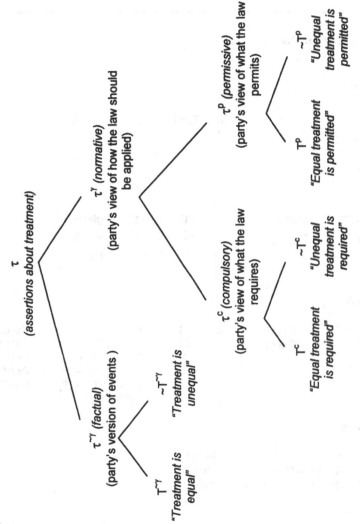

τ
(assertions about treatment)

τ⁻ᵞ *(factual)*
(party's version of events)

Tᵞ
"Treatment is equal"

~Tᵞ
"Treatment is unequal"

τᵞ *(normative)*
(party's view of how the law should be applied)

τᶜ *(compulsory)*
(party's view of what the law requires)

Tᶜ
"Equal treatment is required"

~Tᶜ
"Unequal treatment is required"

τᵖ *(permissive)*
(party's view of what the law permits)

Tᵖ
"Equal treatment is permitted"

~Tᵖ
"Unequal treatment is permitted"

7 Compound Positions

Having developed notation forms for both factual and normative assertions about treatment, we can now record positions which include both kinds of assertions.

7.1 Conjunctions

In *Dothard*, the claimant's factual position [A: $\sim T^{\sim\gamma}$] and normative position [A: T^c] can be joined to form one combined position,

A: $\sim T^{\sim\gamma} \cdot T^c$ *"The treatment is unequal, but should be equal."*

The compound Z position can be stated in the same way. Z concedes factual inequality of treatment [Z: $\sim T^{\sim\gamma}$], asserting that such inequality is permissible [Z: $\sim T^p$],

Z: $\sim T^{\sim\gamma} \cdot \sim T^p$ *"The treatment is unequal, and that unequal treatment is permissible."*

We can say that a θ position combining both a factual assertion and a normative assertion takes the *general form* (GF),

GF. 7-1 $\theta: \tau^{\sim\gamma} \cdot \tau^\gamma$

We can now state in precise terms the difference between the A and Z positions with respect to treatment. One way of doing that is to use only compulsory and non-compulsory assertions,

A: $\sim T^{\sim\gamma} \cdot T^c$ Z: $\sim T^{\sim\gamma} \cdot T^{\sim c}$

Alternatively, we can use only permissive and non-permissive assertions, such that the disagreement can be shown to focus on the normative status of equal treatment.

47

On that (identical) reading, the claimant asserts that *un*equal treatment is prohibited, and the respondent asserts that it is permitted,

$$A: \sim T^{\sim\gamma} \cdot \sim T^{\sim p} \qquad Z: \sim T^{\sim\gamma} \cdot \sim T^{p}$$

Exercise Set 7-1

1. *Derive* θ: $\tau^{\sim\gamma} \cdot \tau^{p}$ *from* Z: $\sim T^{\sim\gamma} \cdot \sim T^{p}$.
2. *Derive* θ: $\tau^{\sim\gamma} \cdot \tau^{\gamma}$ *from* Z: $T^{\sim\gamma} \cdot \sim T^{p}$.
3. *Derive* θ: $\tau^{\sim\gamma} \cdot \tau^{\gamma}$ *from* A: $\sim T^{\sim\gamma} \cdot T^{c}$.

7.2   Alternative Formulas

Sometimes the question whether treatment is equal or unequal is purely semantic, depending on the level of generality at which the claim is pitched. That point is illustrated by a famous case brought before the European Court of Human Rights, the *Belgian Linguistic* case.[1] The case was brought by French-speaking claimants who complained about compulsory Dutch-language education in public schools in the country's Flemish regions. Five of the six regions were recognized in law as Dutch speaking. (Only the Kraainem region maintained a special statutory status.)

The complaint alleged violation of several Convention provisions, of which two are relevant here. First, the claimants alleged a violation of Protocol 1, article 2, which reads in part, "[i]n the exercise of any functions which it assumes in relation to education and to teaching, the State shall respect the right of parents to ensure such education and teaching in conformity with their own religious and philosophical convictions." The Court rejected the idea that this passage obliges the State to observe parents' linguistic preferences.[2] What is relevant for our purposes, however, is that the claimants further alleged a violation of the Convention's non-discrimination guarantee, set forth in article

---

[1] Case "Relating to Certain Aspects of the Laws on the Use of Languages in Education in Belgium," 6 Eur. Ct. H.R. (ser. A) (1968).
[2] *Id.* at 31.

14, *as applied to* Protocol 1, article 2.[3] The Court rejected that claim as well (except as applied to Kraainem).[4]

With respect to the non-discrimination claim, the claimants' argument could be formulated in two different ways,

(i) If the French-speaking and Dutch-speaking pupils are understood as being dissimilarly situated with respect to language (and with respect to the sense of culture and identity to which language is bound), then the complaint alleges that *equal* treatment of all students, by subjecting all students to education in the Dutch language, is discriminatory. With respect to language of instruction, the Francophone claimants seek *un*equal treatment—not in the sense of "inferior" treatment, but in the sense of "not identical" treatment.

(ii) By contrast, if the French-speaking pupils are understood as similarly situated to Dutch speakers with respect to their interest in receiving education in their mother tongue, then the claim amounts to a complaint about *un*equal treatment: Dutch-speaking pupils receive education in their mother tongue, while French-speaking pupils do not. From that perspective, the French speakers seek *equal* treatment.

Thus it cannot be asserted in the abstract either that the claimants seek equal treatment $[A: T^c]$ or that they seek unequal treatment $[A: \sim T^c]$. Either formulation may be appropriate, depending on what is meant by "equal treatment" or "unequal treatment" in each case. The treatment (τ) can be expressed in either of two ways, which are substantively identical but formally distinct. We will label these τ_i and τ_{ii}. One formulation (τ_i) can be expressed in terms of "language of instruction." A second formulation (τ_{ii}) can be expressed in terms of "instruction in one's mother tongue." Thus for τ_i, the claimant's factual position is,

A_i: $T^{\sim\gamma}$ *"The treatment is equal (all are receiving instruction in the same language)."*

The claimant's corresponding normative position is,

---

[3] Recall that, under article 14, complaints of discrimination can be brought only with respect to "the rights and freedoms set forth in this Convention," i.e., with respect to a substantive interest expressly protected by some other Convention article. See, e.g., Van Dijk and Van Hoof, 1998: 711-16.

[4] 6 Eur. Ct. H.R. (ser. A) at 42-44, 49-51, 60-61, 85-87.

A_i: $\sim T^c$ *"The treatment should be unequal (French speakers should receive a different language of instruction from that of Dutch speakers)."*

Hence the compound A_i position,

A_i: $T^{\sim\gamma} \cdot \sim T^c$ *"The treatment is equal, but should be unequal."*

By contrast, for τ_2, the claimant's factual position is,

A_{ii}: $\sim T^{\sim\gamma}$ *"The treatment is unequal (Dutch speakers are receiving instruction in their mother tongue, but French speakers are not)."*

The correlative normative position is,

A_{ii}: T^c *"The treatment should be equal (French speakers should have equal opportunity to receive instruction in their mother tongue)."*

Hence the compound A_{ii} position,

A_{ii}: $\sim T^{\sim\gamma} \cdot T^c$ *"The treatment is unequal, but should be equal."*

    To the State's assertion that there is no discrimination, insofar as all pupils, albeit in the Dutch language, receive equal education[5], the claimants respond with the A_i position: "Yes, there is equal treatment; however, what is required in this case is *un*equal treatment—French-language instruction for French speakers."[6] To the State's assertion that the claimants are seeking a right to "special" treatment not required under the terms of the Convention[7], the claimants respond with the A_{ii} position: "It is only equal treatment—equal opportunity of both language groups for education in their own mother tongue—that is sought."[8]

    The respective positions of the respondent State can be represented in similar fashion. Z_i can designate the State's rejection of A_i. For τ_i, the State's factual assertion is that all pupils are treated equally (hence agreement between the parties on the factual assertion),

---

[5] *Id.* at 21, 58-59, 77-80.
[6] Cf. *id.* at 19-20, 22, 24, 57-58, 75-77.
[7] *Id.* at 20, 22-23, 24, 47-48, 66-68.
[8] Cf. *id.* at 19-20, 37, 46-47, 64-66.

Z_i: $T^{-\gamma}$ *"The treatment is equal (all are receiving instruction in the same language)."*

The State's corresponding normative assertion is that it is permissible for all pupils to be treated equally,

Z_i: T^p *"It is permissible for treatment to be equal (i.e., for French speakers and Dutch speakers to receive the same language of instruction)."*

Hence the compound Z_i position,

Z_i: $T^{-\gamma} \cdot T^p$ *"Treatment is equal, and that equality is permissible."*

For τ_{ii}, the State agrees on the factual assertion that pupils are treated unequally,

Z_{ii}: $\sim T^{-\gamma}$ *"Treatment is unequal (Dutch speakers are receiving instruction in their mother tongue, but French speakers are not)."*

The State's correlative normative assertion is that it is permissible for French speakers to be treated unequally,

Z_{ii}: $\sim T^p$ *"It is permissible for treatment to be unequal (there is no right of French speakers to instruction in their mother tongue—Dutch speakers do not receive Dutch-language education as a matter of right, but only as a matter of State prerogative[9]—thus there is no right to be enjoyed equally)."*

Hence the compound Z_{ii} position,

Z_{ii}: $\sim T^{-\gamma} \cdot \sim T^p$ *"The treatment is unequal, and that inequality is permissible."*

Hereinafter, in order to refer to these various positions generated in *Belgian Linguistic*, we will refer to BL_i and BL_{ii}. In order to refer to positions of the respective parties, we will refer to *BL* A and *BL* Z, and, where necessary, to *BL* A$_i$, *BL* A$_{ii}$, *BL* Z$_i$, or *BL* Z$_{ii}$.

---

[9] *Id.* at 42.

7.3   Breach

The ultimate aim of a claimant's position is to argue that some non-discrimination norm has been *breached* (or *violated*—we will use these two terms interchangeably). Similarly, the aim of the respondent's position is to argue that the non-discrimination norm has *not* been breached. An assertion that some non-discrimination norm has been breached will be denoted by means of the letter B. An assertion that the norm has not been breached will be denoted by means of the symbol ~B. Where it is useful to speak of an assertion of breach or non-breach generally, without further specifying B or ~B, the letter β (beta) will be used,

$$Ps(\beta) \quad \beta \subset B, \sim B$$

In *Dothard*, for example, the claimant's assertions about treatment thus serve as *premises* to the *conclusion* that the Equal Protection clause has been breached. We will use a "double arrow" ($\Rightarrow$) to represent the relationship between the premises and the conclusion of an argument,

$$A: \sim T^\gamma \cdot T^c \Rightarrow B$$

The respondent replies that the claimant is indeed treated unequally, *and* that such treatment is permissible, hence no breach,

$$Z: \sim T^\gamma \cdot \sim T^p \Rightarrow \sim B$$

Exercise Set 7-2

For the Belgian Linguistic *case, write arguments about breach or non-breach of the non-discrimination norm:*

1. *For the A_i position.*   2. *For the Z_i position.*
3. *For the A_{ii} position.*   4. *For the Z_{ii} position.*

We can thus adopt a set of *general treatment formulas* stating the legal consequences that are asserted in conjunction with assertions about treatment,

---
General Treatment Formulas

A: $\sim T^{\gamma} \cdot T^c \Rightarrow B$ 　　　　　　Z: $\sim T^{\gamma} \cdot \sim T^p \Rightarrow \sim B$

A: $T^{\gamma} \cdot \sim T^c \Rightarrow B$ 　　　　　　Z: $T^{\gamma} \cdot T^p \Rightarrow \sim B$

At a higher level of abstraction, we can say that all arguments in discrimination disputes follow the general form,

$$\theta: \tau^{\gamma} \cdot \tau^{\gamma} \Rightarrow \beta$$

Yet those formulas still provide only a rudimentary framework for arguments about discrimination. We will not return to the concept of breach until much later, after we have examined in greater detail the premises of A and Z positions.

Answers to Exercises

Exercise Set 7-1

1. (1) $Z: \sim T^{\gamma} \cdot \sim T^p$ given
   (2) $\theta: \sim T^{\gamma} \cdot \sim T^p$ Ps(θ)
   (3) $\theta: \tau^{\gamma} \cdot \sim T^p$ Ps(τ^{γ})
   ∴ $\theta: \tau^{\gamma} \cdot \tau^p$ Ps(τ^p)

2. (1) $Z: T^{\gamma} \cdot \sim T^p$ given
   (2) $\theta: \sim T^{\gamma} \cdot \sim T^p$ Ps(θ)
   (3) $\theta: \tau^{\gamma} \cdot \sim T^p$ Ps(τ^{γ})
   ∴ $\theta: \tau^{\gamma} \cdot \tau^{\gamma}$ Th(τ^{γ})

3. (1) $A: \sim T^{\gamma} \cdot T^c$ given
   (2) $\theta: \sim T^{\gamma} \cdot T^c$ Ps(θ)
   (3) $\theta: \tau^{\gamma} \cdot T^c$ Ps(τ^{γ})
   ∴ $\theta: \tau^{\gamma} \cdot \tau^{\gamma}$ Th(τ^{γ})

Exercise Set 7-2

1. $A_i: T^{\gamma} \cdot \sim T^c \Rightarrow B$
3. $A_{ii}: \sim T^{\gamma} \cdot T^c \Rightarrow B$

2. $Z_i: T^{\gamma} \cdot T^p \Rightarrow \sim B$
4. $Z_{ii}: \sim T^{\gamma} \cdot \sim T^p \Rightarrow \sim B$

PART II

OBJECTIVE STATUS

8 Revised Factual Positions

An assertion of equal or unequal treatment is only meaningful in discrimination discourse in conjunction with the ascription to some individual of what we will call an *objective status*. Familiar examples include race, ethnicity, religion, language, sex, sexual orientation, age or disability, but many others are possible. In this chapter, we will see that every objective status represents some *set* of elements comprised of at least two *subsets*. A discrimination dispute concerns the treatment of one subset as compared with another.

8.1 Sets and Subsets

Arguments about objective status are arguments about the needs, merits, interests or abilities of members of a class as such, without any individualized attention to a particular member. In *Dothard*, the State's assertion of the inferior capacity of women to perform the requisite tasks is based not on any determination about Ms. Rawlinson's ability, but on its views about the abilities of women in general, within this specific context of a high-security, all-male prison. In *Belgian Linguistic*, the State's assessment of the interests of French-speaking pupils is based not on any particular pupil's circumstances, but on the status or interests of francophone pupils in general. We can therefore define a discrimination claim a bit more precisely as an assertion about treatment *with respect to some objective status*.[1]

An objective status can be understood as a *set* of elements which divide into more than one relevant *subset*. In *Dothard*, the objective status of sex presupposes more than one relevant sex. The set "sex" encompasses the relevant subsets "male sex" and "female sex." In *Belgian Linguistic*, the objective status of language presupposes more than one relevant language: the set "language" encompasses the relevant subsets "Dutch language" and "French language" (better still: the set "language group" encompasses the relevant subsets "Dutch speakers" and "French speakers"). A discrimination claim presupposes that one subset is favored over another.[2]

---

[1] This is not yet a final characterization. Cf. chs. 11-13 *infra*.

[2] On the inevitable presence of comparison between classes in discrimination disputes, see, e.g., Banton, 1999: 110-15. It is sometimes suggested that discrimination on grounds of pregnancy differs from other forms of discrimination by not presupposing any comparitor. That is certainly true if comparitors are drawn only from conventional classifications. The classification "men" fails, since non-pregnant women, too, presumably receive favored treatment. However, as argued in the remainder of this section, comparitors are not to be found only among conventional categories. In some cases, for example, the apposite

Objective status is not limited to such familiar sets as race, ethnicity, religion, language or sex. The sets and subsets relevant to the identification of an objective status can be characterized in countless ways.[3] The fact that an objective status is unconventional will not necessarily undermine its substantive merit. Under the German constitution, for example, the article 3(1) right to equal protection (*Gleichheitssatz*) has been invoked to cover a variety of unfamiliar classifications.[4] An interesting example arose in a 1996 case (hereinafter the *Dutch Pensioner* case) decided by the Constitutional Court.[5] A man born in the Netherlands, and maintaining Dutch citizenship, had lived and worked in West Germany from 1958 to 1968. In 1969, he moved to East Germany, where he worked until attaining the retirement age of 65 in 1985, and where he continued to live until German unification. After unification, legislation was introduced for the purpose of harmonizing retirement pay. However, under the new regulations, as the claimant had already been retired before that legislation came into force, he could not benefit from it. Instead, he was subject to earlier legislation, which denied increased retirement pay to persons who, albeit having worked in West Germany, had established their primary residence in East Germany at the time they reached retirement age.[6]

It was not merely on the basis of foreign nationality—which, like race, sex or religion, is a common classification in discrimination law—that the claimant brought the complaint. That might have been the grounds for his claim had he complained of discrimination as between foreigners and Germans. However, that was not the basis of the complaint, since the older regulation applied equally to Germans—i.e., to Germans who had worked in West Germany, then moved to the East. The relevant classification was more narrowly defined. The claimant alleged that he was treated unequally in comparison to other foreigners who had worked in West Germany—including foreigners who had then moved to some country other than East Germany, and who were still entitled to retirement pay. In other words, the complaint envisaged the objective status of "foreign workers," which included a subset of "foreign workers who had moved to East Germany" vis-à-vis the more favored subset of "foreign workers who had *not* moved to East Germany."[7]

Consider some other examples. In 1964, federal legislation was passed in the United States which provided that food stamps would be issued to needy persons,

---

classifications would be "pregnant persons" and "non-pregnant persons." Admittedly, that division does not express the element of sexism as overtly as does the distinction between the categories "men" and "women." However, it by no means precludes that element, as the category of "pregnancy" is as historically laden with sexism as is the concept of "woman." See generally Townshend-Smith, 1998: ch. 7; Zimmer *et al.*, 1997: 594-627.

[3] Non-discrimination clauses in international instruments drafted after the Second World War commonly include express reference to classifications not expressly named. See, e.g., the "other status" clause of ECHR art. 14. Cf. van Dijk and van Hoof, 1998: 730.

[4] Bleckmann, 1997: 644-45.

[5] 95 BVerfGE 143 (1996).

[6] *Id.* at 148.

[7] *Id.* at 149.

but which denied benefits to "any household containing an individual who is unrelated to any other member of the household."[8] Under that regulation, a number of poor people who would otherwise have qualified were refused benefits. The provision was examined by the Supreme Court in *United States Dept. of Agriculture v. Moreno*,[9] where the claimants argued that the statutory exclusion amounted to a denial of equal protection. Given the set of "households," the statute favored the subset of "households . . . whose members are related to one another," and disfavored the subset of "households containing one or more members who are unrelated to the rest."[10]

Similarly, in *Allegheny Pittsburgh Coal Co. v. County Commission*,[11] the Court examined a complaint brought by a landowner, alleging that her property had been taxed at an unfairly high rate in comparison with other, generally comparable land. The disparity arose when her land was repeatedly assessed at its recent purchase price, while the rate assessed for land which had not been purchased recently had changed little over time, and thus no longer reflected current market value. Given the set of "real property," the complaint envisaged a subset of property recently purchased, and receiving inferior treatment, as compared to the subset of property not recently purchased.[12]

8.2 Terminology

In *Dothard*—as in, *mutatis mutandis, Dutch Pensioner, Moreno* and *Pittsburgh Coal*—the claimant's argument [A: $\sim T^{\gamma} \cdot T^{c}$] presupposes that, within the set "sex," the subset "men" is treated better than the subset "women," with respect to the relevant treatment. Similarly, in *Belgian Linguistic*, the claimants' arguments presuppose that the subset "Dutch speakers" is treated better than the subset "French-speakers."

Let us state those ideas more precisely. The claimants' positions in *Dothard* A, *Dutch Pensioner* A, *Moreno* A, *Pittsburgh Coal* A, and *BL* A_{ii} (we will examine *BL* A_i shortly) assert that,

(a) There is unequal treatment *despite* equality of objective status; and,

(b) There should be equal treatment *on the basis of* equality of objective status.

The phrases "equality of objective status" and "inequality of objective status" are a bit cumbersome. Wherever possible, we will use the shorter phrases, "equal

---

[8] Food Stamp Act of 1964, as amended, 7 U.S.C. § 2012 (e) (1964).
[9] 413 U.S. 528 (1973).
[10] *Id.* at 529 (1973).
[11] 488 U.S. 336 (1989).
[12] On the question of sheer administrative classifications, see Section 14.5 *infra*.

objective status" and "unequal objective status," or, even more simply, "objective equality" and "objective inequality." Claims (a) and (b) can thus be stated more tersely,

(a') There is unequal treatment *despite* objective equality; and,

(b') There should be equal treatment *on the basis of* objective equality.

8.3   Notation

The symbol O will be used to denote an assertion of objective equality; and the symbol ~O, to denote an assertion of objective inequality. Where it is useful to speak of objective status in general, without specifying its value as representing objective equality (O) or inequality (~O), the Greek letter o (omicron) will be used. Hence,

$Ps(o)$ $o \subset O, ~O$

The claimant's factual position in *Dothard* [A: ~T$^\gamma$]—as in *Dutch Pensioner, Moreno* and *Pittsburgh Coal*—asserts that there is unequal treatment in fact despite objective equality [A: O],

A: ~T$^\gamma \cdot$ O   *"The treatment is unequal, despite objective equality."*

Meanwhile, the Z position asserts that there is unequal treatment [Z: ~T$^\gamma$], on the basis of objective *in*equality,[13]

Z: ~T$^\gamma \cdot$ ~O   *"The treatment is unequal, on the basis of objective inequality."*

Again, alternative formal expressions of a claim need not entail contradictions in the substance of the claim. In *Belgian Linguistic*, the claimants assert both objective inequality and objective equality, depending on the formal expression of the corresponding treatment. Two respective values of o (o$_i$, o$_{ii}$) correlate to the respective values of τ (τ$_i$, τ$_{ii}$). Thus, for *BL* A$_i$ [A$_i$: T$^\gamma$], o$_i$ represents an assertion of objective inequality [A: ~O],

A$_i$: T$^\gamma \cdot$ ~O   *"The treatment is equal (all are receiving instruction in the same language), **despite objective inequality of French speakers and Dutch speakers**."*

---

[13] On the status of such locutions as "despite" and "on the basis of," recall Section 1.6, note 10 *supra*.

For *BL* A_{ii} [A_{ii}: ~$T^{-\gamma}$], o_{ii} represents an assertion of objective equality [A: O],

A_{ii}: ~$T^{-\gamma} \cdot O$ *"The treatment is unequal (Dutch speakers are receiving instruction in their mother tongue, but French speakers are not), despite objective equality of French speakers and Dutch speakers."*

For *BL* Z_i [Z_i: $T^{-\gamma}$], o_i represents an assertion of objective equality [Z: O],

Z_i: $T^{-\gamma} \cdot O$ *"The treatment is equal (all are receiving instruction in the same language), on the basis of objective equality of French speakers and Dutch speakers."*

And for *BL* Z_{ii} [Z_{ii}: ~$T^{-\gamma}$], o_{ii} represents an assertion of objective inequality [A: ~O],

Z_{ii}: ~$T^{-\gamma} \cdot \sim O$ *"The treatment is unequal (Dutch speakers are receiving mother-tongue instruction, but French speakers are not), on the basis of objective inequality of Dutch speakers and French speakers with respect to such instruction."*

Given those more precise formulations, a more general form for factual positions can be stated,

GF. 8-1 θ: $\tau^{-\gamma} \cdot o$

Recall the diagram of factual positions that was drawn for Exercise Set 6-5, problem 1, and its incorporation within the larger schema in problem 2. We can now include assertions about objective status as part of factual assertions about treatment,

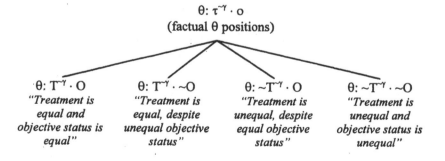

Exercise Set 8-1

1.   *Derive* θ: $\tau^{\gamma} \cdot o$ *from* A: $\sim T^{\gamma} \cdot O$.
2.   *Derive* θ: $\tau^{\gamma} \cdot o$ *from* Z: $\sim T^{\gamma} \cdot \sim O$.

Answers to Exercises

Exercise Set 8-1

1.   (1)   A: $\sim T^{\gamma} \cdot O$ given
     (2)   θ: $\sim T^{\gamma} \cdot O$ Ps(θ)
     (3)   θ: $\tau^{\gamma} \cdot O$ Ps(τ^{γ})
     ∴   θ: $\tau^{\gamma} \cdot o$ Ps(o)

2.   (1)   Z: $\sim T^{\gamma} \cdot \sim O$ Given
     (2)   θ: $\sim T^{\gamma} \cdot \sim O$ Ps(θ)
     (3)   θ: $\tau^{\gamma} \cdot \sim O$ Ps(τ^{γ})
     ∴   θ: $\tau^{\gamma} \cdot o$ Ps(o)

9 Revised Normative Positions

In this chapter, claims about objective status are incorporated into normative arguments about treatment.

9.1   The Conditional Relationship

The claimant's normative position in *Dothard* and BL_{ii} asserts compulsory equal treatment [A: T^c] on the basis of equal objective status [A: O]. That is, the claimant asserts that objective equality provides a *sufficient condition* for compulsory equal treatment: "If the objective status is equal, then the treatment should be equal." We can therefore replace the normative formula A: T^c with the more precise normative formula A: $O \rightarrow T^c$. More compact readings, which we will adopt wherever possible, would be: "equal objective status requires equal treatment," or simply, "objective equality requires equal treatment" (see Figure 9-1).

The party invoking that argument need not assert objective equality (between men and women, or language groups, or domiciles of foreign workers, or kinds of households, or purchase dates of real property) *for all purposes*, but only with respect to the treatment relevant to the dispute: the claimant in *Dothard* need not argue that men and women are alike in all respects, but only with respect to ability to work as guards in high-security prisons; the claimants in *Belgian Linguistic* need not argue that French-speakers and Dutch-speakers are alike in all respects, but only with respect to educational needs and interests relative to language of instruction.

At first glance, a proposition taking the form A: $O \rightarrow T^c$ might appear suspect, as it seems to raise the age-old problem of deriving a value from a fact—deriving a "should" from an "is". Recall, however, that we are not assessing the truth, validity or persuasiveness of such formulas. We are simply pinpointing their structure. Legal rules, and arguments about them, are unthinkable without some derivation of values from facts: "The contract *was* breached, therefore Mary *should be* compensated"; "John *does* possess a valid deed, therefore he *should be* entitled to occupy the land."

The Z position in *Dothard* and BL_{ii} [Z: ~T^p] responds that, if objective status is unequal, it is *permissible* to administer or to tolerate unequal treatment: objective inequality (~O) provides a sufficient condition ($\rightarrow$) for permissive inequality of treatment (~T^p), hence Z: ~$O \rightarrow$ ~T^p. Another way to say that (we will treat the two versions as synonymous) is to say that if objective status is unequal, then unequal treatment is *justified*; or, more concisely, "objective inequality justifies unequal treatment."

In short, then, arguments of the form θ: o $\rightarrow$ τ^{γ} can be read in two ways.

(a) Arguments of the form o $\rightarrow$ τ^{c} can be read: o *requires* τ. Hence, O $\rightarrow$ T^{c} would read: "objective equality requires equal treatment"; ~O $\rightarrow$ ~T^{c} would read: "objective inequality requires unequal treatment".[1]

(b) Arguments of the form o $\rightarrow$ τ^{p} can be read: o *justifies* τ. Hence, O $\rightarrow$ T^{p} would read: "objective equality justifies equal treatment"; and ~O $\rightarrow$ ~T^{p} would read: "objective inequality justifies unequal treatment".[2]

---

[1] Theoretically, the general form o $\rightarrow$ τ^{c} would also allow for assertions of the form ~O $\rightarrow$ T^{c} or O $\rightarrow$ ~T^{c}. In practice, however, such assertions would be absurd. As to the form ~O $\rightarrow$ T^{c}, there is no dispute in which any party would have occasion to assert that objective inequality as such requires equal treatment. Certainly, in many cases, one might appear to argue that treatment should be equal *despite* objective inequality. For example, members of a minority religious group might eagerly defend the proposition that their religion is different from others, and that they are, to that same extent, unequal. However, if they assert that some form of treatment, such as access to education or employment, should be equal, then it is insofar as there is some objective equality, e.g., equal need for or ability in education or employment *despite* those differences, hence O $\rightarrow$ T^{c}.
   Similarly, as to the form O $\rightarrow$ ~T^{c}, no party would have occasion to assert that equal objective status as such requires unequal treatment. Certainly, in many cases, one might appear to argue that treatment should be *unequal* despite objective equality. Again, members of a minority religious group might argue that they require special—and in that sense, unequal—treatment in one respect, despite meriting equal treatment in other respects. However, such an argument assumes that the special treatment is based on a particular objective difference, and, in that sense, on an objective inequality, such as a distinct dietary regime or educational prohibition. In theory, then, the arguments ~O $\rightarrow$ T^{c} and O $\rightarrow$ ~T^{c} are possible, but, in practice, would not arise. We can therefore assume that o $\rightarrow$ τ^{c} will always take either the form O $\rightarrow$ T^{c} or the form ~O $\rightarrow$ ~T^{c} (see Figure 9-1).

[2] Again, theoretically, the general form o $\rightarrow$ τ^{p} allows for assertions of the form O $\rightarrow$ ~T^{p} or ~O $\rightarrow$ T^{p}. In a real discrimination dispute, however, no party would have occasion to make such arguments. As to the form O $\rightarrow$ ~T^{p}, just as no party would assert that equal objective status as such *requires* unequal treatment (O $\rightarrow$ ~T^{c}), nor would a party assert that equal objective status as such *justifies* unequal treatment. Unequal treatment is deemed to be justified insofar as it is based on some relevant, *un*equal status, i.e., notwithstanding any equality of objective status with respect to forms of treatment *other* than those at issue. Similarly, as to the form ~O $\rightarrow$ T^{p}, just as no party would assert that unequal objective status as such *requires* equal treatment (~O $\rightarrow$ T^{c}), nor would a party assert that unequal objective status as such *justifies* equal treatment. Equal treatment is deemed to be justified insofar as it is based on some relevant, equal status, notwithstanding any *in*equality of objective status with respect to forms of treatment other than those at issue. Accordingly, we can assume that o $\rightarrow$ τ^{p} will always take either the form O $\rightarrow$ T^{p} or the form ~O $\rightarrow$ ~T^{p} (see Figure 9-1).

9.2 Schema of Normative Positions

The symbols O and ~O in assertions of the form $o \rightarrow \tau^\gamma$ are not themselves modified by a γ marker, as they signify assertions that are factual in form ('X's *are* equal to Y's'; 'X's *are* unequal to Y's'). The meaning of a value of o in a normative assertion will be identical to its meaning in the factual assertion to which it is correlated. There is no need to label it to indicate whether it is normative or factual, as it is always (formally) factual. In factual assertions, it forms part of the formula θ: $\tau^{\gamma} \cdot o$. In normative assertions, it forms part of the formula θ: $o \rightarrow \tau^\gamma$. For *Dothard, Dutch Pensioner, Moreno, Pittsburgh Coal* or BL_{ii}, A's normative assertion [A: T^c] can now be written as,

A: $O \rightarrow T^c$ *"Objective equality requires equal treatment."*

Z's normative position [Z: ~T^p] becomes,

Z: ~$O \rightarrow$ ~T^p *"Objective inequality justifies unequal treatment."*

By contrast, for *BL* A_i [A_i: ~T^c],

A_i: ~$O \rightarrow$ ~T^c *"Objective inequality requires unequal treatment."*

And *BL* Z_i [Z_i: T^p] becomes,

Z_i: $O \rightarrow T^p$ *"Objective equality justifies equal treatment."*

The general formula θ: τ^γ can thus be revised to provide a more precise general formula for normative positions,

GF. 9-1 θ: $o \rightarrow \tau^\gamma$

Figure 9-1 revises the normative, right-hand branch of θ positions appearing in Figure 4-1 (cf. also Exercise 6-5, problem 2).

Exercise Set 9-1

1. *Derive θ: $o \rightarrow \tau^\gamma$ from A: $O \rightarrow T^c$.*
2. *Derive θ: $o \rightarrow \tau^\gamma$ from Z: ~$O \rightarrow$ ~T^p.*
3. *Derive θ: $o \rightarrow \tau^\gamma$ from Z: $O \rightarrow T^p$.*

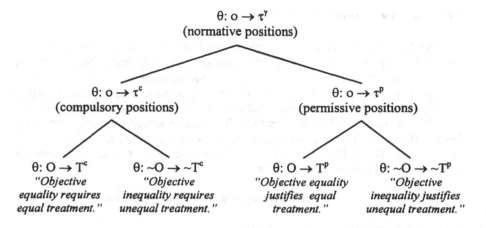

Figure 9-1

Answers to Exercises

Exercise Set 9-1

1. (1) A: O → T^c given
    (2) θ: O → T^c Ps(θ)
    (3) θ: o → T^c Ps(o)
    ∴   θ: o → τ^γ Th(τ^γ)

2. (1) Z: ~O → ~T^p given
    (2) θ: ~O → ~T^p Ps(θ)
    (3) θ: o → ~T^p Ps(o)
    ∴   θ: o → τ^γ Th(τ^γ)

3. (1) A: O → T^p given
    (2) θ: O → T^p Ps(θ)
    (3) θ: o → T^p Ps(o)
    ∴   θ: o → τ^γ Th(τ^γ)

10 Revised Compound Positions

In this chapter, factual and normative claims about treatment and objective status are incorporated into revised compound positions.

10.1 The General Revised Form

For *Dothard, Dutch Pensioner, Moreno, Pittsburgh Coal* and BL_{ii}, we can revise the claimants' earlier compound position $[A: \sim T^{\sim \gamma} \cdot T^c]$ by joining the revised factual component $[A: \sim T^{\sim \gamma} \cdot O]$ to the revised normative component $[A: O \rightarrow T^c]$,

$$A: (\sim T^{\sim \gamma} \cdot O) \cdot (O \rightarrow T^c)$$

Note that O appears twice. In both places, it represents an assertion of objective equality, but that does not make the duplication redundant. The normative position is conditional. It asserts that treatment must be equal *if* objective status is equal. The factual position complements that element by asserting that the condition is fulfilled, that objective status *is* indeed equal. Similarly, Z's position $[Z: \sim T^{\sim \gamma} \cdot \sim T^p]$ can be revised by joining the factual position $[Z: \sim T^{\sim \gamma} \cdot \sim O]$ to the normative position $[Z: \sim O \rightarrow \sim T^p]$,

$$Z: (\sim T^{\sim \gamma} \cdot \sim O) \cdot (\sim O \rightarrow \sim T^p)$$

BL A_i $[A_i: T^{\sim \gamma} \cdot \sim T^c]$ can be revised as,

$$A_i: (T^{\sim \gamma} \cdot \sim O) \cdot (\sim O \rightarrow \sim T^c)$$

BL Z_i $[Z_i: T^{\sim \gamma} \cdot T^p]$ can be revised as,

$$Z_i: (T^{\sim \gamma} \cdot O) \cdot (O \rightarrow T^p)$$

Hence a revised compound general form for θ positions,

GF.10-1 $\theta: (\tau^{\sim \gamma} \cdot o) \cdot (o \rightarrow \tau^\gamma)$

67

Exercise Set 10-1

From the following arguments, derive the general position
θ: $(\tau^{\neg\gamma} \cdot o) \cdot (o \to \tau^{\gamma})$.

Example: A: $(\sim T^{\neg\gamma} \cdot O) \cdot (O \to T^c)$

(1)	A: $(\sim T^{\neg\gamma} \cdot O) \cdot (O \to T^c)$	given
(2)	θ: $(\sim T^{\neg\gamma} \cdot O) \cdot (O \to T^c)$	Ps(θ)
(3)	θ: $(\tau^{\neg\gamma} \cdot O) \cdot (O \to T^c)$	Ps($\tau^{\neg\gamma}$)
(4)	θ: $(\tau^{\neg\gamma} \cdot o) \cdot (o \to T^c)$	Ps(o)
$\therefore$	θ: $(\tau^{\neg\gamma} \cdot o) \cdot (o \to \tau^{\gamma})$	Th(τ^{γ})

1. Z: $(T^{\neg\gamma} \cdot O) \cdot (O \to T^c)$
2. A: $(T^{\neg\gamma} \cdot \sim O) \cdot (\sim O \to \sim T^c)$
3. Z: $(\sim T^{\neg\gamma} \cdot \sim O) \cdot (\sim O \to \sim T^p)$
4. Z: $(T^{\neg\gamma} \cdot O) \cdot (O \to T^p)$

10.2   Compound Positions and Syllogistic Form

Let us examine more closely the relationship between the factual and normative components of the compound position. Again, the normative position asserts that treatment should be equal *if* objective status is equal. The factual position complements that assertion, affirming that objective status *is* indeed equal. The relationship between the factual and the normative components can then be represented in vertical syllogistic form. We see that that the combination of the factual premise O with the normative premise O $\to$ T^c results in the conclusion T^c, which is normative,

A's normative premise	A: O $\to$ T^c	*If* objective status is equal, *then* treatment should be equal.
A's factual premise	A: O	Objective status *is* equal.
A's normative conclusion	A: T^c	Treatment should be equal

Figure 10-1

Exercise Set 10-2

For each problem in Exercise Set 10-1 *construct syllogisms in vertical form which display the party's normative conclusion.*

Example: θ: (~T$^{\gamma}$ · O) · (O → T^c)

Answer:

normative premise	θ: O → T^c
factual premise	θ: O

---

normative conclusion	θ: T^c

Although the factual assertion about treatment (~T$^{\gamma}$) does not appear in Figure 10-1, it can nevertheless be inserted for the sake of completeness, to provide a more accurate picture of the claimant's position. It takes on a somewhat inert character, as a non-essential premise, but is worth including insofar as it provides a means of noting the distinction between the claimant's factual and normative assertions about treatment,

A's factual premise	A: ~T$^{\gamma}$	Treatment is unequal
A's normative premise	A: O → T^c	*If* objective status is equal, *then* treatment should be equal.
A's factual premise	A: O	Objective status *is* equal.

A's normative conclusion	A: T^c	Treatment should be equal

The claimant's three premises in that calculation can be combined to form one compound premise,

A's factual and normative premise	A: ~T$^{\gamma}$ · (O → T^c) · O

A's normative conclusion	A: T^c

We can tidy things up by grouping the elements of the premise so as to distinguish more clearly its factual from its normative components,

A's factual and normative premise   A: $(\sim T^{\gamma} \cdot O) \cdot (O \to T^c)$

A's normative conclusion   A: T^c

If we replace the conclusion line with a symbol separating the premises from the conclusion, we can dispense altogether with the vertical notation form. We have seen that the double arrow ($\Rightarrow$) serves that purpose,

A: $[(O \cdot \sim T^{\gamma}) \cdot (O \to T^c)] \Rightarrow T^c$

Exercise Set 10-3

For each problem in Exercise Set 10-1, construct syllogisms in horizontal form, including the full compound position, which display the party's normative conclusion.

Example: θ: $(\sim T^{\gamma} \cdot O) \cdot (O \to T^c)$
Answer: θ: $[(\sim T^{\gamma} \cdot O) \cdot (O \to T^c)] \Rightarrow T^c$

Answers to Exercises

Exercise Set 10-1

1. (1) Z: $(T^{\gamma} \cdot O) \cdot (O \to T^c)$ given
   (2) θ: $(T^{\gamma} \cdot O) \cdot (O \to T^c)$ Ps(θ)
   (3) θ: $(\tau^{\gamma} \cdot O) \cdot (O \to T^c)$ Ps(τ^{γ})
   (4) θ: $(\tau^{\gamma} \cdot o) \cdot (o \to T^c)$ Ps(o)
   ∴ θ: $(\tau^{\gamma} \cdot o) \cdot (o \to \tau^{\gamma})$ Th(τ^{γ})

2. (1)   A: $(T^{\gamma} \cdot \sim O) \cdot (\sim O \rightarrow \sim T^c)$ given
   (2)   θ: $(T^{\gamma} \cdot \sim O) \cdot (\sim O \rightarrow \sim T^c)$ Ps(θ)
   (3)   θ: $(\tau^{\sim\gamma} \cdot \sim O) \cdot (\sim O \rightarrow \sim T^c)$ Ps($\tau^{\sim\gamma}$)
   (4)   θ: $(\tau^{\sim\gamma} \cdot o) \cdot (o \rightarrow \sim T^c)$ Ps(o)
   ∴   θ: $(\tau^{\sim\gamma} \cdot o) \cdot (o \rightarrow \tau^{\gamma})$ Th(τ^{γ})

3. (1)   Z: $(\sim T^{\gamma} \cdot \sim O) \cdot (\sim O \rightarrow \sim T^p)$ given
   (2)   θ: $(\sim T^{\gamma} \cdot \sim O) \cdot (\sim O \rightarrow \sim T^p)$ Ps(θ)
   (3)   θ: $(\tau^{\sim\gamma} \cdot \sim O) \cdot (\sim O \rightarrow \sim T^p)$ Ps($\tau^{\sim\gamma}$)
   (4)   θ: $(\tau^{\sim\gamma} \cdot o) \cdot (o \rightarrow \sim T^p)$ Ps(o)
   ∴   θ: $(\tau^{\sim\gamma} \cdot o) \cdot (o \rightarrow \tau^{\gamma})$ Th(τ^{γ})

4. (1)   Z: $(T^{\gamma} \cdot O) \cdot (O \rightarrow T^p)$ given
   (2)   θ: $(T^{\gamma} \cdot O) \cdot (O \rightarrow T^p)$ Ps(θ)
   (3)   θ: $(\tau^{\sim\gamma} \cdot O) \cdot (O \rightarrow T^p)$ Ps($\tau^{\sim\gamma}$)
   (4)   θ: $(\tau^{\sim\gamma} \cdot o) \cdot (o \rightarrow T^p)$ Ps(o)
   ∴   θ: $(\tau^{\sim\gamma} \cdot o) \cdot (o \rightarrow \tau^{\gamma})$ Th(τ^{γ})

Exercise Set 10-2

1. normative premise   Z: $O \rightarrow T^c$
    factual premise   Z: O

    ---

    normative conclusion   Z: T^c

2. normative premise   A: $\sim O \rightarrow \sim T^c$
    factual premise   A: $\sim O$

    ---

    normative conclusion   A: $\sim T^c$

3. normative premise   Z: $\sim O \rightarrow \sim T^p$
    factual premise   Z: $\sim O$

    ---

    normative conclusion   Z: $\sim T^p$

4.   normative premise   Z: O → T^p
     factual premise   Z: O

_____

     normative conclusion   Z: T^p

Exercise Set 10-3

1.   Z: [(T$^\gamma$ · O) · (O → T^c)] ⇒ T^c
2.   A: [(T$^\gamma$ · ~O) · (~O → ~T^c)] ⇒ ~T^c
3.   Z: [(~T$^\gamma$ · ~O) · (~O → ~T^p)] ⇒ ~T^p
4.   Z: [(T$^\gamma$ · O) · (O → T^p)] ⇒ T^p

PART III

SUBJECTIVE MERIT

11 Final Normative Positions

Only by including the element of *subjective merit*—consisting of some particular determination of ability, need or circumstances—can we adequately account for the structure of discrimination discourse. In this chapter, the formulas developed thus far are further refined in order to take subjective merit into account.

11.1 Notation

In *Dothard*, the argument A: $O \rightarrow T^c$ does not fully account for the claimant's normative position. As we have seen, the claimant does not, and need not, argue that women and men are equal in all ways or for all purposes. She does not argue that the objective status of "woman" suffices in itself to require equal treatment with men. Rather, limiting her argument to the question of qualification to serve as a prison guard, she refers more specifically to subjective merit—to her ability to perform the tasks required for the job. She argues that she possesses something that we will call *commensurate subjective merit*—that is, individual ability, intelligence and education which meet, which are *commensurate with*, the requirements of the job. She thus advocates equal treatment of women and men not *regardless* of individual ability to perform the tasks in question, but *because* of it, i.e., *insofar as* it is present in her case.

An assertion of *commensurate subjective merit*—an assertion that one possesses some ability or need which should entitle one to enjoy a benefit from which, under the challenged rule, one is barred—will be represented by the letter S. Accordingly, an assertion of *incommensurate subjective merit*—an assertion that one *does not* possess some ability or need which should entitle one to enjoy that benefit—will be represented by the letter ~S. Where it is useful to speak of subjective merit in general, without specifying it as being commensurate (S) or incommensurate (~S), the Greek symbol σ (sigma) will be used,

Ps(σ)   σ ⊂ S, ~S.

Like O and ~O, the symbols S and ~S are unmodified by any γ or ~γ marker, as they represent only assertions about subjective merit that are formally factual.

Once again, the phrase *"formally* factual" is crucial. Like questions of equality or inequality of objective status, substantive questions of individual merit, ability or need involve value judgments, and are not factual in any transcendental sense. In *Dothard*, both the claimant and the respondent make formally factual assertions ("A woman can perform the tasks without posing an increased danger to

75

herself or to the prison regime"; "A woman can*not* perform the tasks without posing an increased danger to herself or to the prison regime"), each relying on their own mixtures of legal norms, empirical data and cultural values.

11.2 Normative Assertions

The claimant in *Dothard* must stake out a middle position between two extremes. She need not assert that women and men are equal for all purposes, but only with respect to the specific treatment at issue—competence to serve as a guard. Nor however can she assert that commensurate subjective merit is itself sufficient to require equal treatment [A: $S \rightarrow T^c$], as the law is full of inequalities of treatment on the basis of objective status despite the existence of some individuals whose subjective merit might otherwise qualify them for equal treatment. The fact that some individual 10-year-olds might be sophisticated (commensurate subjective merit) at forming contracts is not generally recognized as rendering a uniform, higher age requirement (objective status) invalid.

Rather, the claimant argues that her commensurate ability to perform the requisite tasks suffices to establish sexual equality for purposes of hiring prison guards. That is, she argues that commensurate subjective merit provides a sufficient condition for a finding of objective equality *in that case*: *if* there is commensurate subjective merit with respect to the requisite tasks, *then* there is objective equality as between women and men with respect to those tasks. (By analogy, sophisticated children, seeking an equal right to enter into contracts, might bring a discrimination claim along the same lines. They would have to argue that their commensurate subjective merit provides a sufficient condition for a finding of objective equality as between adults and sophisticated children for purposes of contract formation: *if* there is commensurate subjective merit with respect to contract formation, *then* there is objective equality as between adults and sophisticated children for that purpose. In reality, of course, skepticism about the meaning of "sophisticated" would likely doom such a claim.) In *Dothard*, then, the claimant's argument is structured as follows,

(a) Commensurate subjective merit (ability to perform the tasks without posing an increased danger to herself or to the prison regime) provides a sufficient condition for a finding of objective equality (of women and men), for purposes of hiring a prison guard [A: $S \rightarrow O$].

(b) Objective equality (of women and men) provides a sufficient condition for compulsory equal treatment [A: $O \rightarrow T^c$].

That structure follows the rule of hypothetical syllogism,[1] and can be represented as follows,

---

[1] See Section 4.6. n. 9, *supra*.

factual premise   A: S → O

normative premise   A: O → T^c

normative conclusion   A: S → T^c

The concluding position A: S → T^c omits O, but *only insofar* as O was essential to its derivation: the claimant asserts that commensurate subjective merit suffices to require equal treatment, *but only insofar* as commensurate subjective merit suffices to establish objective equality for purposes of the relevant treatment.[2] For the sake of economy, the syllogism can be written horizontally,

F.11-1   A: [(S → O) · (O → T^c)] ⇒ (S → T^c)

As compared with the formula A: O → T^c, that formula displays a more complete statement of the claimant's normative position.

Now consider the State's position. Recall that the State authorities focus not on the claimant's individual abilities, but on the overall climate of an all-male, high-security penitentiary, which, they claim, is unsuitable for women *per se*. On that view, the sheer fact of being a woman entails an inequality in objective status; that objective inequality in turn provides a sufficient condition for a finding of incommensurate merit for *any* particular woman: *if* there is objective inequality as between women and men with respect to the requisite tasks, *then* there is *ipso facto* incommensurate subjective ability on the part of any particular woman to perform the tasks without posing an increased danger to herself or to the prison regime. That argument is structured as follows,

(a) Objective inequality (of women and men) provides a sufficient condition for a finding of incommensurate subjective merit (inability of any given woman) to perform the tasks in this case [Z: ~O → ~S].

(b) Incommensurate subjective merit (inability of any given woman to perform the tasks without posing an increased danger to herself or to the prison regime)

---

[2] Those familiar with formal logic may wonder whether some element of quantification is relevant here. Objective status represents characteristics attributed to a class of individuals, while subjective merit corresponds to characteristics of specified individuals within a class. For example, assume that W represents women, Q represents qualification to serve as a prison guard, (∀x) represents the class of "all x", and (∃x) represents "some (particular) x". The State authorities can then be said to argue Z: (∀x)(Wx → ~Qx), while the claimant argues A: (∃x)(Wx · Qx). While those notation forms might serve a more advanced analysis, they are not sufficiently useful to require further examination here.

justifies—i.e., provides a sufficient condition for—unequal treatment [Z: $\sim S \to \sim T^p$].

Hence,

factual premise $\qquad$ Z: $\sim O \to \sim S$

normative premise $\qquad$ Z: $\sim S \to \sim T^p$

_____

normative conclusion $\qquad$ Z: $\sim O \to \sim T^p$

The concluding position Z: $\sim O \to \sim T^p$ omits $\sim S$, but *only insofar* as $\sim S$ was essential to its derivation: the State asserts that objective inequality suffices to justify unequal treatment, *but only insofar* as objective inequality suffices to establish incommensurate subjective merit with respect to any given woman, for purposes of the relevant treatment. The syllogism can be written horizontally,

F.11-2 $\quad$ Z: $[(\sim O \to \sim S) \cdot (\sim S \to \sim T^p)] \Rightarrow (\sim O \to \sim T^p)$

The conclusion Z: $\sim O \to \sim T^p$ does not differ from the normative position we had already stated for Z, but this new formula as a whole does display the role of subjective merit.

Consider some other examples. In *Moreno*, the claimants argue that their level of poverty is equal to that of households which, containing only related members, are eligible to receive food stamps; hence an assertion of commensurate subjective merit. They argue that the purpose of the food stamp program is to reduce malnutrition among indigent persons; their commensurate subjective merit therefore renders the objective status of "households containing one or more unrelated individuals" equal to the objective status of "households containing only related individuals." Accordingly,

(a) Commensurate subjective merit (need based on indigence) provides a sufficient condition for a finding of objective equality (between households containing, and those not containing, unrelated individuals) for purposes of alleviating malnutrition among poor people [A: $S \to O$];

(b) Objective equality (between households containing, and those not containing, unrelated individuals) provides a sufficient condition for compulsory equal treatment [A: $O \to T^c$].

Exercise Set 11-1

For Moreno, *apply the rule of hypothetical syllogism to derive A's normative conclusion:*

1. In vertical form
2. In horizontal form

Now consider the Z position. Under the original 1964 Food Stamp Act, the term "household" had been defined to encompass both related and non-related individuals.[3] Concern subsequently arose in Congress that individuals, notably hippies and hippie communes, were forming households for the sole purpose of collecting food stamps. The Act was amended in 1971, as Justice Rehnquist stated, to limit the meaning of "household" to "some variation of the family as we know it . . . exist[ing] for some purpose other than to collect federal food stamps."[4] Justice Rehnquist conceded that Congress had "attacked the problem with a rather blunt instrument,"[5] and that the limitation would "have unfortunate and perhaps unintended consequences"[6] for some persons in genuine need. He nevertheless supported the government view in defence of the constitutionality of the amendment, arguing that "equal protection analysis does not require that every classification be drawn with precise 'mathematical nicety.'"[7] He thus endorsed the government position that households containing more than one unrelated individual comported a greater risk of fraudulent use of food stamps[8] and, for purposes of the Act, could rationally be deemed unequal to households not containing more than one unrelated individual.[9]

For the government, then, the increased risk of fraud comported by the class of "households containing two or more unrelated individuals" entailed an objective inequality of that class vis-à-vis the class of "households containing only related individuals." That risk was great enough to dispose of the question of the individual subjective merit of any particular household within that class. That is, the risk was great enough to warrant a finding that the objective inequality of the class itself provided a sufficient condition for a finding of incommensurate subjective merit of any given household of that class,

---

[3] 78 Stat 703. Cf. 413 U.S. 528, 530 (1973).

[4] 413 U.S. at 546 (Rehnquist, J., dissenting).

[5] *Id.* at 545.

[6] *Id.* at 547.

[7] *Id.* at 546. Cf. the Court opinion, *id.* at 538 (citing Dandridge v. Williams, 397 U.S. 471, 485 (1970)).

[8] 413 U.S. at 546 (Rehnquist, J., dissenting).

[9] *Id.* at 546, 547.

(a) The risk of fraud is such that objective inequality (between households containing, and those not containing, unrelated individuals) provides a sufficient condition for a finding of incommensurate subjective merit (i.e., even if indigence is taken into account) [Z: $\sim O \rightarrow \sim S$];

(b) Incommensurate subjective merit provides a sufficient condition for discretionary unequal treatment [Z: $\sim S \rightarrow \sim T^p$].

Exercise Set 11-2

For Moreno, *apply the rule of hypothetical syllogism to derive Z's normative conclusion:*

1. In vertical form
2. In horizontal form

In *Dutch Pensioner*, the State authorities do not dispute the fact that the individual claimant had indeed completed ten years of work in West Germany. Rather, they argue that East Germany's retirement law had already encompassed periods of work completed in West Germany. An entitlement to a West German pension would have meant that pensioners would receive double retirement pay for any work completed in West Germany. In the government's view, that fact distinguished the entire class of foreign workers who had emigrated to East Germany from foreign workers who had not done so. Hence an objective inequality which distinguished the work completed by the individual claimant from work completed by foreigners who did not receive East German pensions,[10]

(a) Objective inequality (between foreign workers who had, and those who had not, emigrated to East Germany) provides a sufficient condition for a finding of incommensurate subjective merit (arising from individual work performed) [Z: $\sim O \rightarrow \sim S$];

(b) Incommensurate subjective merit (arising from individual work performed) provides a sufficient condition for discretionary unequal treatment [Z: $\sim S \rightarrow \sim T^p$].

---

[10] 95 BVerfGE 143, 156 (1996).

Exercise Set 11-3

For Dutch Pensioner, *apply the rule of hypothetical syllogism to derive Z's normative conclusion:*

1. In vertical form
2. In horizontal form

The claimant in *Dutch Pensioner*, however, argued that work duly completed when he had lived in West Germany, hence commensurate subjective merit, rendered his objective status as a foreigner who had emigrated to East Germany equal, for purposes of the dispute, to the status of foreign workers who had not emigrated to East Germany,

(a) Commensurate subjective merit (arising from individual work performed) provides a sufficient condition for a finding of objective equality (between foreign workers who had, and those who had not, emigrated to East Germany) [A: S → O];

(b) Objective equality (between foreign workers who had, and those who had not, emigrated to East Germany) provides a sufficient condition for compulsory equal treatment [A: O → T^c].

Exercise Set 11-4

For Dutch Pensioner, *apply the rule of hypothetical syllogism to derive A's normative conclusion:*

1. In vertical form
2. In horizontal form

The A and Z positions generated for BL_{ii} correlate to those we have ascertained for *Dothard, Moreno* and *Dutch Pensioner*. The claimants (BL A_{ii}) need not establish that French-speaking and Dutch-speaking pupils are equal for all purposes. Rather, the parents assert that it is their children's individual needs to receive instruction in their mother tongue which render them equal to Dutch pupils. The claimants argue that "'children may encounter serious difficulty in learning

Dutch'."[11] They demand for their children "an education which 'will best ensure the fullest development of [their] personalit[ies]', by means of conditions in conformity with [their] 'abilities' and 'emotions'."[12] In other words, commensurate subjective merit, in terms of individual educational and cultural needs, provides a sufficient condition for a finding of objective equality between the two language groups,

(a) Commensurate subjective merit (of educational and cultural needs) provides a sufficient condition for a finding of objective equality (of French-speaking and Dutch-speaking pupils) [A_{ii}: $S \rightarrow O$];

(b) Objective equality (of French-speaking and Dutch-speaking pupils) provides a sufficient condition for compulsory equal treatment [A_{ii}: $O \rightarrow T^c$].

Hence the horizontal formula,

F.11-3 A_{ii}: $[(S \rightarrow O) \cdot (O \rightarrow T^c)] \Rightarrow (S \rightarrow T^c)$

On the government's side (*BL* Z_{ii}), the Court notes that the claimants have provided no actual evidence of French-speaking children incurring any disadvantages.[13] The government argues that there simply does not exist any legally compelling claim on the State to receive education in one's mother tongue;[14] that the resulting bilingualism (francophone pupils exposed to French at home and Dutch in school), far from causing any disadvantage, provides the children with a positive advantage, both educationally and in later professional life.[15] In the government's view, Dutch speakers in Dutch-speaking regions enjoy the possibility of education in their mother tongue, so to speak, as a democratic windfall—as a benefit of their majority presence in the Flemish areas—and not as a matter of right.[16] Equal claims on rights do not extend to equal claims on windfalls, with respect to which the minority French speakers living in Dutch-speaking regions are indeed collectively—objectively—unequal to Dutch speakers,

(a) Objective inequality (vis-à-vis a claim to education in one's mother tongue) provides a sufficient condition for a finding of incommensurate subjective merit (despite actual or perceived educational or cultural need) [Z_{ii}: $\sim O \rightarrow \sim S$];

---

[11] 6 Eur. Ct. H.R. (ser. A) at 40 (1968).
[12] *Id.* at 24. See also *id.* at 37.
[13] *Id.*
[14] Concerning the application of Protocol 1, article 2 of the Convention, see Section 7.2 *supra.*
[15] *Id.* at 38.
[16] *Id.* at 42.

(b) Incommensurate subjective merit (despite actual or perceived educational or cultural need) provides a sufficient condition for discretionary unequal treatment [Z_{ii}: ~S → ~T^p].

Hence the formula,

F.11-4 Z_{ii}: [(~O → ~S) · (~S → ~T^p)] ⇒ (~O → ~T^p)

Alternatively, in *BL* A$_i$, the claimants seek to assert that equal treatment—instruction in the Dutch language for all pupils—disregards relevant *in*equalities between the two classes of pupils. It is not because French speakers are different from Dutch speakers that they have different needs. Rather, it is because—and only insofar as—they have different needs that they are different from Dutch speakers. From that perspective, the claimants assert objective *in*equality between French and Dutch speakers—not for all purposes, but only for purposes of language of instruction. For *BL* A$_i$, then, *in*commensurate subjective merit, in terms of educational and cultural need, provides a sufficient condition for a finding of objective inequality between the two language groups,

(a) Incommensurate subjective merit (different educational and cultural needs) provides a sufficient condition for a finding of objective inequality (of French-speaking and Dutch-speaking pupils) [A$_i$: ~S → ~O];

(b) Objective inequality (of French-speaking and Dutch-speaking pupils) provides a sufficient condition for compulsory unequal treatment [A$_i$: ~O → ~T^c].

Exercise Set 11-5

For Belgian Linguistic, *apply the rule of hypothetical syllogism to derive a normative conclusion for A$_i$:*

1. In vertical form
2. In horizontal form

The State's response (*BL* Z$_i$) is that, for purposes of language of instruction, there is objective equality between the two groups. As French speakers have no peremptory claim to French as a language of instruction, no individual French-speaking pupil, as such, has any particular need for treatment different from that accorded to Dutch-speaking pupils. (As the case involved issues of general educational arrangements, it was not principally concerned with exceptional circumstances, such as the needs of pupils with specific learning disabilities, who might have a distinct interest in receiving education in their mother tongue.)

(a) Objective equality (of French-speaking and Dutch-speaking pupils) provides a sufficient condition for a finding of commensurate subjective merit (of educational and cultural need) [Z_i: O → S];

(b) Commensurate subjective merit (of educational and cultural need) provides a sufficient condition for discretionary equal treatment [Z_i: S → T^p].

Exercise Set 11-6

For Belgian Linguistic, *apply the rule of hypothetical syllogism to derive a normative conclusion for Z_i:*

1. In vertical form
2. In horizontal form

In *Dothard, Moreno, Dutch Pensioner* and *Belgian Linguistic*, the A positions are drawn largely from the specific circumstances of the actual claimants. Indeed, in some jurisdictions, that would be indispensable. In the United States, for example, federal courts adhere to "case or controversy" and "ripeness" doctrines,[17] which preclude review of government action or legislation in the abstract. But assume that the legal rules complained of in any of those cases had arisen in jurisdictions which allow some form of judicial review in the abstract—in the form of advisory, or even binding, opinions. In the absence of identified claimants, what kind of arguments could be made about subjective merit?

Presumably, the arguments would be the same. For example, in a case based on the disputed regulation in *Dothard*, a court could simply postulate the existence of a woman qualified to perform the requisite tasks. That would be a necessary, even if only implicit, step: what else would it mean to decide that a legal rule is or is not discriminatory? To decide that a legal rule is or is not discriminatory is to decide that there is some individual—either already ascertained, or ascertainable in principle—who, in comparison to other individuals, would be unfairly affected by that rule. In a case like *Moreno*, such a court would either expressly or implicitly postulate the existence of deserving households; in *Dutch Pensioner*, the court would postulate the existence of a foreign worker who had completed a period of work in West Germany before emigrating to East Germany; and so forth. The existence of actual claimants in these cases provides only an illustrative, but not an indispensable, basis for challenging the allegedly discriminatory rules. That is also

---

[17] Nowak and Rotunda, 2000: 64-107.

why the model developed in this book applies regardless of differences in the status of doctrines of precedent or *stare decisis*, i.e., regardless of differences in the status of judicial opinions in common law and civil law jurisdictions.

In *Dothard, Moreno, Dutch Pensioner* and BL_{ii}, we see that the relationships between τ, o and σ in the A and Z positions, respectively, are identical. Only in BL_i are the symbols different. At a hierarchically superior level, however, we can identify formulas which unite all of the A and Z positions, respectively, in all of the foregoing cases,

F.11-5   A: $[(\sigma \rightarrow o) \cdot (o \rightarrow \tau^\gamma)] \Rightarrow (\sigma \rightarrow \tau^\gamma)$

F.11-6   Z: $[(o \rightarrow \sigma) \cdot (\sigma \rightarrow \tau^\gamma)] \Rightarrow (o \rightarrow \tau^\gamma)$

Exercise Set 11-7

Derive the following formulas.

Example: Derive F.11-5 from F.11-1.

(1)	A: $[(S \rightarrow O) \cdot (O \rightarrow T^c)] \Rightarrow (S \rightarrow T^c)$	given (F.11-1)
(2)	A: $[(\sigma \rightarrow O) \cdot (O \rightarrow T^c)] \Rightarrow (\sigma \rightarrow T^c)$	Ps(σ)
(3)	A: $[(\sigma \rightarrow o) \cdot (o \rightarrow T^c)] \Rightarrow (\sigma \rightarrow T^c)$	Ps(o)
∴	A: $[(\sigma \rightarrow o) \cdot (o \rightarrow \tau^\gamma)] \Rightarrow (\sigma \rightarrow \tau^\gamma)$	Ps(τ^γ)

1. *Derive F.11-6 from F.11-2.*
2. *Derive F.11-5 from F.11-3.*
3. *Derive F.11-6 from F.11-4.*

Yet even at that higher level of abstraction, F.11-5 and F.11-6 do not represent every kind of discrimination dispute. They represent only what we will later call the "traditional" discrimination dispute. We will see that there are other possible configurations of τ, o and σ, representing other kinds of controversies.

11.3   Simplified Positions

The formulas in F.11-1 through F.11-6 are complete insofar as they display the party's full normative premises and conclusions. Recall, however, that the normative position is only part of the party's larger argument—which also includes a factual position. Later on, it will be time again to merge these revised factual and normative positions into compound positions. But it will be unduly cumbersome, and unnecessary, to use such long formulas. As long as we now know how the conclusion has been deduced from the premises in the full normative positions in F.11-1 through F.11-6, we can simply use the conclusion as a simplified statement of the full normative position. Thus, for example, F.11-1 can be stated as follows,

F.11-1'   A: S → T^c

Exercise Set 11-8

Write simplified normative positions for F.11-2 to F.11-6.

Answers to Exercises

Exercise Set 11-1

1.   factual premise   A: S → O

     normative premise   A: O → T^c

     _____

     normative conclusion   A: S → T^c

2.   A: [(S → O) · (O → T^c)] ⇒ (S → T^c)

Exercise Set 11-2

1   factual premise   Z: $\sim O \rightarrow \sim S$

      normative premise   Z: $\sim S \rightarrow \sim T^p$

---

      normative conclusion Z: $\sim O \rightarrow \sim T^p$

2.   Z: $[(\sim O \rightarrow \sim S) \cdot (\sim S \rightarrow \sim T^p)] \Rightarrow (\sim O \rightarrow \sim T^p)$

Exercise Set 11-3

1   factual premise   Z: $\sim O \rightarrow \sim S$

      normative premise   Z: $\sim S \rightarrow \sim T^p$

---

      normative conclusion Z: $\sim O \rightarrow \sim T^p$

2.   Z: $[(\sim O \rightarrow \sim S) \cdot (\sim S \rightarrow \sim T^p)] \Rightarrow (\sim O \rightarrow \sim T^p)$

Exercise Set 11-4

1.   factual premise   A: $S \rightarrow O$

      normative premise   A: $O \rightarrow T^c$

---

      normative conclusion A: $S \rightarrow T^c$

2.   A: $[(S \rightarrow O) \cdot (O \rightarrow T^c)] \Rightarrow (S \rightarrow T^c)$

Exercise Set 11-5

1. factual premise A_i: ~S → ~O

    normative premise A_i: ~O → ~T^c

    _____

    normative conclusion A_i: ~S → ~T^c

2. A_i: [(~S → ~O) · (~O → ~T^c)] ⇒ (~S → ~T^c)

Exercise Set 11-6

1. factual premise Z_i: O → S

    normative premise Z_i: S → T^p

    _____

    normative conclusion Z_i: O → T^p

2. Z_i: [(O → S) · (S → T^p)] ⇒ (O → T^p)

Exercise Set 11-7

1.   (1)   Z: [(~O → ~S) · (~S → ~T^p)] ⇒ (~O → ~T^p)   given (F.11-2)
     (2)   Z: [(o → ~S) · (~S → ~T^p)] ⇒ (o → ~T^p)   Ps(o)
     (3)   Z: [(o → σ) · (σ → ~T^p)] ⇒ (σ → ~T^p)   Ps(σ)
     ∴   Z: [(o → σ) · (σ → τ^γ)] ⇒ (o → τ^γ)   Ps(τ^γ)

2.   (1)   A: [(S → O) · (O → T^c)] ⇒ (S → T^c)   given (F.11-3)
     (2)   A: [(σ → O) · (O → T^c)] ⇒ (σ → T^c)   Ps(σ)
     (3)   A: [(σ → o) · (o → T^c)] ⇒ (σ → T^c)   Ps(o)
     ∴   A: [(σ → o) · (o → τ^γ)] ⇒ (σ → τ^γ)   Ps(τ^γ)

3. (1)   Z: $[(\sim O \to \sim S) \cdot (\sim S \to \sim T^p)] \Rightarrow (\sim O \to \sim T^p)$ given (F.11-4)
    (2)   Z: $[(o \to \sim S) \cdot (\sim S \to \sim T^p)] \Rightarrow (o \to \sim T^p)$ Ps(o)
    (3)   Z: $[(o \to \sigma) \cdot (\sigma \to \sim T^p)] \Rightarrow (\sigma \to \sim T^p)$ Ps(σ)
    ∴   Z: $[(o \to \sigma) \cdot (\sigma \to \tau^\gamma)] \Rightarrow (o \to \tau^\gamma)$ Ps(τ^γ)

Exercise Set 11-8

F.11-2'   Z: $\sim O \to \sim T^p$ F.11-3' A_{ii}: $S \to T^c$
F.11-4' Z_{ii}: $\sim O \to \sim T^p$ F.11-5'   A: $\sigma \to \tau^\gamma$
F.11-6'   Z: $o \to \tau^\gamma$

12 Final Factual Positions

Having developed final normative positions, we will now use the relationship between objective status and subjective merit to develop final factual positions.

12.1 General Logical Forms

Before pursuing our examination of actual cases, let us take a moment to examine some further elements of logical form. Consider the following formula,

> F.12-1 $[(p \rightarrow q) \cdot p] \Rightarrow q$

We have already seen that this configuration represents a classic syllogism,

$$(1) \quad p \rightarrow q$$
$$(2) \quad P$$
$$\therefore \quad Q$$

That form of syllogism is central to traditional logic, and is commonly known as *modus ponendo ponens*, or, for short, *modus ponens*.[1] Now consider the following formula,

> F.12-2 $[(p \rightarrow q) \cdot p] \Rightarrow p \cdot q$

The proof of that argument is straightforward,

(1)	$p \rightarrow q$	Given
(2)	p	Given
(3)	q	*modus ponens (applied to steps 1 and 2)*
$\therefore$	$p \cdot q$	conjunction *(applied to steps 2 and 3)*

Finally, consider the formula,

> F.12-3 $[(p \rightarrow q) \cdot p \cdot r] \Rightarrow p \cdot q \cdot r$

The proof is similar,

---

[1] Detlefsen *et al.*, 1999: 67-68.

(1) $p \to q$ given
(2) p given
(3) r given
(4) q *modus ponens (applied to steps 1 and 2)*
(5) $p \cdot q$ conjunction *(applied to steps 2 and 4)*
∴ $p \cdot q \cdot r$ conjunction *(applied to steps 5 and 3)*

Exercise Set 12-1

Write vertical proofs for the following arguments.

1. $[a \cdot (a \to b)] \Rightarrow b \cdot a$
2. $[a \cdot c \cdot (a \to b)] \Rightarrow a \cdot b \cdot c$
3. $[a \cdot (a \to c) \cdot b] \Rightarrow b \cdot c \cdot a$

12.2   Relationship between Objective Status and Subjective Merit

For *Dothard*, we recorded a compound factual position for the claimant by joining her assertion that treatment is unequal [A: $\sim T^{\gamma}$] to her assertion that objective status is equal [A: O],[2]

A: $\sim T^{\gamma} \cdot$ O   *"The treatment is unequal, despite objective equality."*

In the last chapter we saw that the claimant's assertion of objective equality itself derives from a prior factual assertion of commensurate subjective merit: there is objective equality *if* there is commensurate subjective merit [A: S → O]. That is, in order to reach the conclusion that there is in fact objective equality between men and women for purposes of working as a guard [A: O], she must assert that the antecedent condition *is fulfilled*—that *there is* commensurate subjective merit on her part with respect to the requisite tasks [A: S],

---

[2] See Section 8.3 *supra*.

1st factual premise	A: S → O	*If* there is commensurate subjective merit on the part of the claimant, with respect to the requisite tasks, *then* there is objective equality between men and women for purposes of employment as a guard.
2nd factual premise	A: S	There is commensurate subjective merit on the part of the claimant, with respect to the requisite tasks.
factual conclusion	A: O	There is objective equality between men and women for purposes of employment as a guard.

Hence, in horizontal form,

F.12-4   A: [(S → O) · S] ⇒ O

Exercise Set 12-2

The following syllogism represents the claimants' argument in Moreno. *Fill in the blanks.*

1st factual premise	A: __1__ → O	*If* there is commensurate subjective merit on the claimants' part with respect to indigence, *then* there is objective equality between house-holds containing, and households not containing, unrelated members.
2nd factual premise	__2__ : S	There is commensurate __3__ merit on the claimants' part with respect to indigence.
factual conclusion	A: __4__	There is objective __5__ between households containing, and house-holds not containing, unrelated members.

Exercise Set 12-3

The following syllogism represents the claimant's argument in Dutch Pensioner. *Fill in the blanks.*

1st factual premise   A: S → __1__   *If* there is commensurate subjective merit on the claimant's part with respect to work completed in West Germany, *then* there is objective equality between foreign workers who emigrated, and foreign workers who did not emigrate, to East Germany.

2nd factual premise   A: __2__   There is __3__ on the __4__ part with respect to work completed in West Germany.

factual conclusion   __5__   There is __6__ between __7__ .

12.3 Final Positions

For *Dothard, Moreno* and *Dutch Pensioner* (we will examine *Belgian Linguistic* shortly), F.12-4 provides a derivation for the claimants' assertions about objective status from their conceptually prior assertions about subjective merit. A fuller statement of their factual positions runs as follows,

F.12-5   A: $[(S \to O) \cdot S] \Rightarrow S \cdot O$

Exercise Set 12-4

Write a proof for F.12-5 *in vertical form.*

An even more complete statement—the claimants' final factual positions—can be written as follows,

F.12-6   A: $[(S \rightarrow O) \cdot S \cdot \sim T^{\gamma}] \Rightarrow \sim T^{\gamma} \cdot S \cdot O$

Exercise Set 12-5

Write a proof for F.12-6 *in vertical form.*

12.4   Respondents' Positions

For *Dothard*, compare the foregoing arguments with the arguments adduced by the respondent. Recall that we had recorded a factual position for the State authorities by joining their assertion that treatment is unequal $[Z: \sim T^{\gamma}]$ to their assertion that objective status is unequal $[Z: \sim O]$,[3]

> Z: $\sim T^{\gamma} \cdot \sim O$ *"The treatment is unequal, on the basis of objective inequality."*

When we were studying the claimant's position, we saw that her assertion about objective status depended on a prior assertion about subjective merit. We have seen, however, that, for the respondent, the opposite is true. The assertion about subjective merit follows from the assertion about objective status. For the State authorities, the assertion of incommensurate subjective merit follows from the assertion of unequal objective status: *if* there is objective inequality between women and men with respect to ability to perform the tasks of prison guard successfully, *then* there is *ipso facto* incommensurate subjective merit on the part of the claimant to be hired for that position [Z: $\sim O \rightarrow \sim S$],

---

[3] See Section 8.3 *supra*.

1st factual premise	Z: ~O → ~S	*If* there is objective inequality between women and men with respect to ability to perform the tasks of prison guard successfully, *then* there is incommensurate subjective merit on the part of the claimant to be hired for that position.
2nd factual premise	A: ~O	There is objective inequality between women and men with respect to ability to perform the tasks of prison guard successfully.

factual conclusion	A: ~S	There is incommensurate subjective merit on the part of the claimant to be hired for that position.

Hence, in horizontal form,

F.12-7   Z: $[(\sim O \rightarrow \sim S) \cdot \sim O] \Rightarrow \sim S$

Exercise Set 12-6

The following syllogism represents the respondent's argument in Moreno. *Fill in the blanks.*

1st factual premise	Z: __1__ → ~S	*If* there is objective inequality between households containing, and households not containing, unrelated members, with respect to qualification for food stamps, *then* there is incommensurate subjective merit on the claimants' part (despite their indigence).
2nd factual premise	__2__ : ~O	There is objective __3__ between households containing, and households not containing, unrelated members with respect to qualification for food stamps.

Factual conclusion	Z: __4__	There is __5__ subjective __6__ on the claimants' part (despite their indigence).

Exercise Set 12-7

The following syllogism represents the respondent's argument in Dutch Pensioner. *Fill in the blanks.*

1st factual premise	__1__	*If,* with respect to pensions, there is objective inequality between foreign workers who have emigrated, and foreign workers who have not emigrated, to East Germany, *then* there is incommensurate subjective merit on the part of the claimant (despite work completed in West Germany).
2nd factual premise	__2__	With respect to pensions, there is __3__ between __4__ .
Factual conclusion	__5__	There is __6__ on the part of the __7__ (despite work completed in West Germany).

For *Dothard, Moreno* and *Dutch Pensioner*, then, F.12-7 provides a derivation for the respondents' assertions about subjective merit from their logically prior assertions about objective status. A fuller statement of their factual positions runs as follows,

$$\text{F.12-8} \quad Z: [(\sim O \to \sim S) \cdot \sim O] \Rightarrow \sim S \cdot \sim O$$

The respondents' final factual positions can thus be written as follows,

$$\text{F.12-9} \quad Z: [(\sim O \to \sim S) \cdot \sim O \cdot \sim T^{\gamma}] \Rightarrow \sim T^{\gamma} \cdot \sim S \cdot \sim O$$

Exercise Set 12-8

Write a proof for F.12-9 *in vertical form.*

12.5   Alternative Positions

As we have seen, the *Belgian Linguistic* case provides alternative formal expressions for substantively identical positions. The claimants' and respondent's positions in BL_{ii} are identical to those of *Dothard, Moreno* and *Dutch Pensioner*.

Exercise Set 12-9

The following syllogism represents the claimants' argument in BL$_{ii}$.
Fill in the blanks.

1st factual premise	A$_{ii}$: __1__	*If* there is commensurate subjective merit on the part of French-speaking pupils with respect to education in the French language, *then* there is objective equality between French-speaking and Dutch-speaking pupils with respect to education in their mother tongues.
2nd factual premise	__2__	There is __3__ on the part of __4__ with respect to __5__.

factual conclusion	__6__	There is __7__ between __8__ with respect to education in their mother tongues.

Exercise Set 12-10

The following syllogism represents the respondent's argument in BL$_{ii}$.
Fill in the blanks.

1st factual premise	Z$_{ii}$: __1__	*If* there is objective inequality between French-speaking and Dutch-speaking pupils with respect to claims on education in their mother tongues, *then* there is incommensurate subjective merit on the part of French-speaking pupils with respect to education in the French language.
2nd factual premise	__2__	There is __3__ between __4__ with respect to claims on education in their mother tongues.

factual conclusion	__5__	There is __6__ on the part of __7__ with respect to education in the French language.

Recall that, for *BL* A_i, we had recorded a compound factual position by joining the claimants' assertion that treatment is equal [A_i: $T^{\sim\gamma}$] to their assertion objective status is unequal [A_i: $\sim$O],[4]

A_i: $T^{\sim\gamma} \cdot \sim$O   *"The treatment is equal (all are receiving instruction in the same language), despite objective inequality of French speakers and Dutch speakers."*

We have seen, however, that the assertion of objective inequality is itself based on a prior assertion of incommensurate subjective merit [A_i: $\sim$S $\rightarrow$ $\sim$O]. That is, in order to reach the conclusion that there is objective inequality between French-speakers and Dutch-speakers for purposes of education [A_i: $\sim$O], the claimants assert that there is incommensurate subjective merit on the part of francophone children: their educational and cultural needs are different from those of Dutch-speaking children [A_i: $\sim$S].

Exercise Set 12-11

The following syllogism represents the claimants' argument in BL_i. *Fill in the blanks.*

1st factual premise	A_i: __1__	*If* there is incommensurate subjective merit on the part of French-speaking pupils with respect to education in the Dutch language, *then* there is objective inequality between French-speaking and Dutch-speaking pupils with respect to language of education.
2nd factual premise	__2__	There is __3__ on the part of __4__ with respect to __5__ .
factual conclusion	__6__	There is __7__ between __8__ with respect to language of education.

---

[4] See Section 8.3 *supra*.

Exercise Set 12-12

Write a full factual argument for BL A$_l$ in horizontal form.

For *BL Z$_i$*, we had recorded a compound factual position by joining the respondent's assertion that treatment is equal [Z$_i$: T$^{-\gamma}$] to an assertion that objective status is equal [A: O],[5]

Z$_i$: T$^{-\gamma}$ · O   *"The treatment is equal (all are receiving instruction in the same language), on the basis of objective equality of French speakers and Dutch speakers."*

For the State, that assertion of equal objective status entails an assertion of commensurate subjective merit: if there is objective equality between French-speakers and Dutch-speakers with respect to language of instruction (all are receiving instruction in the same language), then there is no *in*commensurate subjective merit on the part of French-speaking pupils which would require any special or different treatment.

Exercise Set 12-13

The following syllogism represents the respondent's argument in BL$_l$. Fill in the blanks.

1st factual premise	Z$_i$: __1__	If there is objective equality between French-speaking and Dutch-speaking pupils with respect to language of education (all are receiving instruction in the same language), *then* there is commensurate subjective merit on the part of French-speaking pupils to be educated in the Dutch language.
2nd factual premise	__2__	There is __3__ between __4__ with respect to language of education.
factual conclusion	__5__	There is __6__ on the part of __7__ to be educated in the Dutch language.

---

[5] See Section 8.3 *supra.*

Exercise Set 12-14

Write a full factual argument for BL Z_1 *in horizontal form.*

12.6   General Positions

Although *Belgian Linguistic* entails alternative formal positions, a general statement of the final factual positions in *Dothard, Moreno, Dutch Pensioner* and *BL*
runs as follows,

F.12-10   A: $[(\sigma \to o) \cdot \sigma \cdot \tau^{\neg\gamma}] \Rightarrow \tau^{\neg\gamma} \cdot \sigma \cdot o$

F.12-11   Z: $[(o \to \sigma) \cdot o \cdot \tau^{\neg\gamma}] \Rightarrow \tau^{\neg\gamma} \cdot \sigma \cdot o$

Exercise Set 12-15

1.   *Derive F.12-10 from F.12-6.*
2.   *Derive F.12-11 from F.12-9.*

12.7   Simplified Positions

Formulas F.12-6, F.12-9, F.12-10 and F.12-11 are complete insofar as they display
the party's full factual premises and conclusions.   Once again, however, the
conclusions can be used to represent the entire argument, in order to allow a
simpler notation form.   For example, F.12-6 can be stated as follows,

F.12-6'   A: $\sim T^{\neg\gamma} \cdot S \cdot O$

Exercise Set 12-16

Write simplified factual positions for F.12-9, F.12-10 *and* F.12-11.

Answers to Exercises

Exercise Set 12-1

1. (1) a   given
   (2) a → b   given
   (3) b   *modus ponens* (applied to steps 1 and 2)
   ∴ b · a   conjunction (applied to steps 3 and 1)

2. (1) a   given
   (2) c   given
   (3) a → b   given
   (4) b   *modus ponens* (applied to steps 1 and 3)
   (5) a · b   conjunction (applied to steps 1 and 4)
   ∴ a · b · c   conjunction (applied to steps 5 and 2)

3. (1) a   given
   (2) a → c   given
   (3) b   given
   (4) c   *modus ponens* (applied to steps 1 and 2)
   (5) b · c   conjunction (applied to steps 3 and 4)
   ∴ b · c · a   conjunction (applied to steps 5 and 1)

Exercise Set 12-2

1. S
2. A
3. subjective
4. O
5. equality

Exercise Set 12-3

1. O
2. S
3. commensurate subjective merit
4. claimant's
5. A: O
6. objective equality
7. foreign workers who emigrated, and foreign workers who did not emigrate, to East Germany

Exercise Set 12-4

(1)	S → O	given
(2)	S	given
(3)	O	*modus ponens* (applied to steps 1 and 2)
∴	S · O	conjunction (applied to steps 2 and 3)

Exercise Set 12-5

(1)	S → O	given
(2)	S	given
(3)	~T˥	given
(4)	O	*modus ponens* (applied to steps 1 and 2)
(5)	~T˥ · S	conjunction (applied to steps 3 and 2)
∴	~T˥ · S · O	conjunction (applied to steps 5 and 4)

Exercise Set 12-6

1. ~O
2. Z
3. inequality
4. ~S
5. incommensurate
6. merit

Exercise Set 12-7

1. Z: ~O → ~S
2. Z: ~O
3. objective inequality
4. foreign workers who have emigrated, and foreign workers who have not emigrated, to East Germany
5. Z: ~S
6. incommensurate subjective merit
7. claimant

Exercise Set 12-8

(1)	~O → ~S	given
(2)	~O	given
(3)	~T˥	given
(4)	~S	*modus ponens* (applied to steps 1 and 2)
(5)	~T˥ · ~S	conjunction (applied to steps 3 and 4)
∴	~T˥ · ~S · ~O	conjunction (applied to steps 5 and 3)

Exercise Set 12-9

1. $S \rightarrow O$
2. A_{ii}: S
3. commensurate subjective merit
4. French-speaking pupils
5. education in the French language
6. A_{ii}: O
7. objective equality
8. French-speaking and Dutch-speaking pupils

Exercise Set 12-10

1. $\sim O \rightarrow \sim S$
2. Z_{ii}: $\sim O$
3. objective inequality
4. French-speaking and Dutch-speaking pupils
5. Z_{ii}: $\sim S$
6. incommensurate subjective merit
7. French-speaking pupils

Exercise Set 12-11

1. $\sim S \rightarrow \sim O$
2. A_i: $\sim S$
3. incommensurate subjective merit
4. French-speaking pupils
5. education in the Dutch language
6. A_i: $\sim O$
7. objective inequality
8. French-speaking and Dutch-speaking pupils

Exercise Set 12-12

A_i: $[(\sim S \rightarrow \sim O) \cdot \sim S \cdot T^\gamma] \Rightarrow T^\gamma \cdot \sim S \cdot \sim O$

Exercise Set 12-13

1. $O \rightarrow S$
2. Z_i: O
3. objective equality
4. French-speaking and Dutch-speaking pupils
5. Z_i: S
6. commensurate subjective merit
7. French-speaking pupils

Exercise Set 12-14

Z_i: $[(O \rightarrow S) \cdot O \cdot T^\gamma] \Rightarrow T^\gamma \cdot S \cdot O$

Exercise Set 12-15

1.   (1)   A: $[(S \to O) \cdot S \cdot {\sim}T^\gamma] \Rightarrow {\sim}T^\gamma \cdot S \cdot O$ given (F.12-6)
      (2)   A: $[(\sigma \to O) \cdot \sigma \cdot {\sim}T^\gamma] \Rightarrow {\sim}T^\gamma \cdot \sigma \cdot O$ Ps(σ)
      (3)   A: $[(\sigma \to o) \cdot \sigma \cdot {\sim}T^\gamma] \Rightarrow {\sim}T^\gamma \cdot \sigma \cdot o$ Ps(o)
    $\therefore$ A: $[(\sigma \to o) \cdot \sigma \cdot \tau^\gamma] \Rightarrow \tau^\gamma \cdot \sigma \cdot o$ Ps(τ^γ)

2,   (1)   Z: $[({\sim}O \to {\sim}S) \cdot {\sim}O \cdot {\sim}T^\gamma] \Rightarrow {\sim}T^\gamma \cdot {\sim}S \cdot {\sim}O$ given (F.12-9)
      (2)   Z: $[(o \to {\sim}S) \cdot o \cdot {\sim}T^\gamma] \Rightarrow {\sim}T^\gamma \cdot {\sim}S \cdot o$ Ps(o)
      (3)   Z: $[(o \to \sigma) \cdot o \cdot {\sim}T^\gamma] \Rightarrow {\sim}T^\gamma \cdot \sigma \cdot o$ Ps(σ)
    $\therefore$ Z: $[(o \to \sigma) \cdot o \cdot \tau^\gamma] \Rightarrow \tau^\gamma \cdot \sigma \cdot o$ Ps(τ^γ)

Exercise Set 12-16

F.12-9'   Z: ${\sim}T^\gamma \cdot {\sim}S \cdot {\sim}O$

F.12-10'   A: $\tau^\gamma \cdot \sigma \cdot o$

F.12-11'   Z: $\tau^\gamma \cdot \sigma \cdot o$

13 Final Compound Positions

In this chapter, we combine the final factual and normative positions in order to generate final compound positions.

13.1 Conjunction of Final Factual and Normative Positions

Recall that we have formed compound positions by conjoining factual and normative positions.[1] We can now do the same with our simplified versions of the revised factual and normative positions. The claimants' positions in *Dothard, Moreno, Dutch Pensioner* and BL_{ii} take the following form (the parentheses around the cluster $\sim T^{\sim \gamma} \cdot S \cdot O$ are not strictly necessary, but are used as an aid to distinguish the factual and normative components),

F.13-1   A: $(\sim T^{\sim \gamma} \cdot S \cdot O) \cdot (S \rightarrow T^c)$

Exercise Set 13-1

1. *Write the respondents' final compound position for* Dothard, Moreno, Dutch Pensioner *and* BL_{ii}.
2. *Write the claimants' final compound position for* BL_i.
3. *Write the respondent's final compound position for* BL_i.
4. *Write general compound A positions for F.11-5 and F.12.10*
5. *Write general compound Z positions for F.11-6 and F.12.11.*

13.2 Eliminating the Conditional Proposition

On closer inspection, we see that F.13-1 can be further simplified. While it includes a conditional proposition $[S \rightarrow T^c]$, it also asserts that the antecedent condition is fulfilled—i.e., it asserts S. We can, then, write a simpler compound position that eliminates the conditional proposition,

---

[1] See Chapters 7 and 10 *supra*.

(1)	$\sim T^{\gamma}$	given
(2)	S	given
(3)	O	given
(4)	$S \rightarrow T^c$	given
(5)	T^c	*modus ponens* (applied to steps 2 and 4)
(6)	$\sim T^{\gamma} \cdot S$	conjunction (applied to steps 1 and 2)
(7)	$\sim T^{\gamma} \cdot S \cdot O$	conjunction (applied to steps 6 and 3)
∴	$\sim T^{\gamma} \cdot S \cdot O \cdot T^c$	conjunction (applied to steps 7 and 5)

It would seem, then, that F.13-1 can take a simpler form, free of any conditional statements,

F.13-2   A: $\sim T^{\gamma} \cdot S \cdot O \cdot T^c$

Or, if we want to continue to keep the factual and normative assertions visibly distinct,

F.13-3   A: $(\sim T^{\gamma} \cdot S \cdot O) \cdot T^c$

In the following chapters, however, we will not use these more simplified forms, as we will see that the inclusion of the conditional assumption provides clearer insight into the distinguishing features of different kinds of arguments.

13.3   Breach

Recall that A and Z positions are themselves premises to arguments that some non-discrimination norm has or has not been breached.[2] F.13-1 can thus be stated more precisely,

F.13-4   A: $[(\sim T^{\gamma} \cdot S \cdot O) \cdot (S \rightarrow T^c)] \Rightarrow B$

Exercise Set 13-2

Re-do Exercise Set 13-1, writing all compound positions as arguments about breach or non-breach.

---

[2] See Section 7.3 *supra*.

Answers to Exercises

Exercise Set 13-1

1. Z: $(\sim T^{\gamma} \cdot \sim S \cdot \sim O) \cdot (\sim S \rightarrow \sim T^{p})$
2. A: $(T^{\gamma} \cdot \sim S \cdot \sim O) \cdot (\sim S \rightarrow \sim T^{c})$
3. Z: $(T^{\gamma} \cdot S \cdot O) \cdot (S \rightarrow T^{p})$
4. A: $(\tau^{\gamma} \cdot \sigma \cdot o) \cdot (\sigma \rightarrow \tau^{\gamma})$
5. Z: $(\tau^{\gamma} \cdot \sigma \cdot o) \cdot (o \rightarrow \tau^{\gamma})$

Exercise Set 13-2

1. Z: $[(\sim T^{\gamma} \cdot \sim S \cdot \sim O) \cdot (\sim S \rightarrow \sim T^{p})] \Rightarrow \sim B$
2. A: $[(T^{\gamma} \cdot \sim S \cdot \sim O) \cdot (\sim S \rightarrow \sim T^{c})] \Rightarrow B$
3. Z: $[(T^{\gamma} \cdot S \cdot O) \cdot (S \rightarrow T^{p})] \Rightarrow \sim B$
4. A: $[(\tau^{\gamma} \cdot \sigma \cdot o) \cdot (\sigma \rightarrow \tau^{\gamma})] \Rightarrow B$
5. Z: $[(\tau^{\gamma} \cdot \sigma \cdot o) \cdot (o \rightarrow \tau^{\gamma})] \Rightarrow \sim B$

PART IV

GENERAL FORMS OF ARGUMENT

14 The Traditional Model

We have thus far examined only one general kind of discrimination dispute, which we will call the *traditional* dispute. Before examining alternatives, however, we will take a closer look at the traditional model.

14.1 General Form

The dispute that we are calling "traditional" arises where the respondent avowedly treats the claimant unequally, based on some objective status. In *Dothard*, *Moreno*, *Dutch Pensioner* and *Belgian Linguistic*, the State in no way denies that the treatment is unequal. Rather, the inequality is expressly stated in law or policy, and defended as such by the State. The claimant challenges the objective inequality, arguing that commensurate subjective merit establishes equal objective status for purposes of the relevant treatment. The parties' disagreement about the values of τ, o and σ thus entails a disagreement about those symbols' formal relationships *inter se*,

$$A: [(\tau^{-\gamma} \cdot \sigma \cdot o) \cdot (\sigma \rightarrow \tau^c)] \Rightarrow B$$

$$Z: [(\tau^{-\gamma} \cdot \sigma \cdot o) \cdot (o \rightarrow \tau^p)] \Rightarrow \sim B$$

14.2 "Classic" Discrimination: The Example of Race

In 1890, the Louisiana State legislature passed a law requiring separate railway carriages for "white" and "colored" passengers. Two years later, Homer Plessy, a man of "mixed" race was imprisoned for refusing to vacate a coach reserved for whites. In the case of *Plessy v. Ferguson*,[1] the United States Supreme Court held that, as long as carriages were provided for persons of all races, the law requiring segregation of the carriages had not violated the Equal Protection clause of the Fourteenth Amendment. With that decision, it adopted the infamous "separate but equal" doctrine, which remained in force for over half a century.

Mr. Plessy's complaint was based in part on the claim that he was "seven eighths Caucasian and one eighth African blood; [and] that the mixture of colored blood was not discernible in him."[2] Although the Court briefly examined the

---

[1] 163 U.S. 537 (1896).
[2] *Id.* at 541.

111

constitutionality of the statute under the Thirteenth Amendment, which prohibited slavery and involuntary servitude, its opinion focused primarily on the Equal Protection Clause of the Fourteenth Amendment. One obvious strategy for Plessy was to construct an argument based on his commensurate need to use public transportation (and, it goes without saying, his commensurate ability and willingness to fulfill the customary requirements of public transport—possession of a valid ticket, proper passenger conduct, and the like). Under the Louisiana statute, train transportation was available to non-whites.[3] For the claimant, the requirements of equal protection went further—and the case turned on this point. Plessy argued that State regulation of public train transportation could be called equal only if it permitted racial integration.[4] Material equality of resources, but which fell short of fully integrated service, amounted to unequal treatment,

$$\text{F.14-1} \quad \text{A:} \ [(\sim T^{\gamma} \cdot S \cdot O) \cdot (S \to T^c)] \Rightarrow B$$

For the State, the requirements of the Equal Protection Clause were fulfilled, as there was general parity of service between the races. That view, however, raised a further question. If the requirement of equal protection could be met by means of a parity which fell short of integration, then there remained in the law some residual measure of inequality. The central issue in the case concerned the constitutionality of that residual inequality. In its normative position, the State had to identify some objective inequality which justified its finding of incommensurate subjective merit,

$$\text{Z:} \ [(\sim O \to \sim S) \cdot (\sim S \to \sim T^p)] \Rightarrow (\sim O \to \sim T^p)$$

In the face of what would appear to be obvious commensurate subjective merit, in terms of need to travel or ability to observe the rules of carriage (F.14-1), what relevant basis could there be for a premise of objective inequality?

The State's position, embraced by the Court in *Plessy*, reflects a view of race not as a cultural construct but as a fact of nature. The Court cites an early Massachusetts case equating racial distinctions with the distinction between the sexes, which, too, is widely accepted as comporting natural differences of need, interest and ability in the 19th century.[5] Similarly, the Court draws an analogy between racial differences and age differences: a principle of absolute equality would yield such absurdities as identical legal rights for children and adults. Yet,

---

[3] *Id.* at 540 (citing Section 1 of the statute).

[4] *Id.* at 542.

[5] 163 U.S. at 544 (discussing Roberts v. City of Boston, 59 Mass. (5 Cush.) 198 (1850)). In the first US Supreme Court case to deal with sex discrimination, the Court upheld a State prohibition on the practice of law by women. See *Bradwell v. Illinois*, 83 U.S. (16 Wall.) 130, 141 (1873) (Bradley, J., concurring on the basis of "[t]he paramount destiny and mission of woman [which] are to fulfill the noble and benign offices of wife and mother. This is the law of the Creator. And the rules of civil society must be adapted to the general constitution of things . . . ."). Cf. Heinze, 1999b: 45-59.

the Court reasoned, objective differences between children and adults are not arbitrary. They correspond to differences of need, interest or ability—that is, to incommensurate subjective merit between children and adults. In the same way, "in the nature of things,"[6] objective differences of race comport intrinsic—for our purposes, subjective—differences. The Court conceded that certain things are unaffected by racial difference. These would presumably include black passengers' equal need to use public transportation, and equal ability to purchase a ticket, to observe rules of passenger conduct, etc. To that same extent, non-whites are allowed to ride on trains. However, the Court found that other things, such as public or social intermingling, *are* affected by racial difference;[7] and that, to the same extent, racial difference entails human difference. In other words, the Court found that racial difference entails some sufficient degree of incommensurate subjective merit, for purposes of access to public amenities, as between whites and non-whites,

$$\text{F.14-2} \quad Z: [(\sim T^{\sim \gamma} \cdot \sim S \cdot \sim O) \cdot (\sim O \rightarrow \sim T^p)] \Rightarrow \sim B$$

Again, our task in this analysis is not to provide substantive commentary—which would require a longer analysis, more expressly rooted in historical and political context.

Only in 1954 did the Supreme Court re-examine the "separate but equal" doctrine. In *Brown v. Board of Education*,[8] claimants from several States complained of racial segregation in the public schools. The respondent States submitted, and the Court, for purposes of the case, accepted the lower-court findings "that the Negro and white schools have been equalized, or are being equalized, with respect to buildings, curricula, qualifications and salaries of teachers, and other 'tangible' factors."[9] The respondent States thus maintained their position in F.14-2: the provision of equal services having fulfilled the requirements of equal protection, any residual racial discrimination fell within the States' prerogatives to govern in the public interest. This time, however, the Court rejected the derivation of *any* incommensurate subjective merit from objective status. It found that racial segregation in itself created an inferior educational environment for black pupils. Fully equal education required not only "tangible" material resources, but also the "intangible" opportunities to share in the full educational experiences available to whites.[10] The Court thus accepted the A position in F.14-1 as applied to all aspects of education, "tangible" as well as "intangible."

---

[6] 163 U.S. at 544.

[7] *Id.* at 544, 550, 551-52.

[8] 347 U.S. 483 (1954).

[9] *Id.* at 492.

[10] *Id.* at 493-94.

14.3 Continuing Controversies: The Example of Sexual Orientation

In a number of recent cases, United States federal courts have sought to determine the constitutionality of the "Don't Ask, Don't Tell" policy, which was adopted for the armed forces under the Clinton administration.[11] Under the policy, persons serving in or seeking to join the armed forces were not to be asked about their sexual orientation, but would remain subject to discharge if they disclosed that they were lesbian or gay. The cases were brought by individuals who had been discharged under the policy for revealing that they were homosexual. Central to their argument was that sexual orientation has no bearing on individual ability to perform military tasks: commensurate subjective merit entails objective equality with respect to the relevant tasks; and objective equality requires equal treatment (F.14-1).

In defending the policy, the federal government has not questioned the individual abilities of gays to perform military tasks. Like the States in *Plessy* and *Brown*, conceding blacks' overall interests in having access to transportation or education, the federal government does not assert that incommensurate subjective merit itself justifies a finding of objective inequality. It asserts the opposite: merely by *being* a homosexual officer—regardless of anything one *does*—one can damage troop cohesion and thus diminish military effectiveness. For the government, the very fact of an individual's homosexuality (unequal objective status), abstracted from any particular fact of individual conduct, itself implies a greater likelihood of disrupting efficient military functioning, thus justifying a finding of incommensurate subjective merit (F.14-2).

The traditional model structures other kinds of claims based on sexual orientation, such as age of consent, employment, housing or inheritance disputes.[12] In *Sutherland v. the United Kingdom*,[13] the European Commission sustained the claimant's challenge to British law setting a higher age of consent to engage in homosexual activity. Defending the higher age of consent as a means "to protect young men from conduct by which they will set themselves apart from the rest of society and which they may well regret when they reach greater maturity,"[14] the government attributed such risks to homosexuality *per se* (F.14-2). The Commission, however, endorsed the claimant's position, noting "current medical opinion . . . to the effect that sexual orientation is fixed in both sexes by the age of 16, and that men aged 16-21 are not in need of special protection because of the risk of their being 'recruited' into homosexuality."[15] Thus characterizing adolescent sexual orientation as a *fait accompli*, the claimant's position does not merely

---

[11] See, e.g., *Phillips v. Perry*, 106 F.3d 1420 (9th Cir. 1997); *Richenberg v. Perry*, 97 F.3d 256 (8th Cir. 1996); *Thomasson v. Perry*, 80 F.3d 915 (4th Cir. 1996); *Able v. United States*, 88 F.3d 1280 (2d Cir. 1996).

[12] See, e.g., Heinze, 1995: chs. 12, 14.

[13] App. No. 25186/94, 24 Eur. Hum. Rts. Rep. (Comm'n Supp.) C.D 22 (1997).

[14] *Id.* at 29, para. 47.

[15] *Id.* at 32, para. 64 (noting also that "the risk posed by predatory older men would appear to be as serious whether the victim is a man or woman").

challenge the likelihood of the risk asserted by the government, but rather undermines the idea that the eventualities in question can credibly be characterized as "risks." For the claimant and the Commission, the objective status of homosexuality entails no such risk. The question of age of consent can thus be decided only with reference to subjective maturity, and not with reference to the objective status of sexual orientation (F.14-1).

14.4 New Classifications and Standards of Judicial Review

Recall that the Fourteenth Amendment to the United States Constitution, adopted in 1868, provides that "[n]o State shall . . . deny to any person within its jurisdiction the equal protection of the laws."[16] It includes no enumeration of protected classes of individuals. In that respect, it differs not only from more recent national legislation, such as the Civil Rights Act of 1964,[17] but also from more recent international, regional and national instruments,[18] which customarily refer to such classifications as race, ethnicity, religion, sex or national origin. The US Supreme Court had at first expressed doubt that the Equal Protection Clause, adopted in the aftermath of the Civil War, would extend to classifications other than race.[19] In recent years, however, the Court has recognized other classifications,[20] including sex,[21] national origin,[22] or birth out of wedlock,[23] as subject to protection under the Clause.

What, exactly, does it mean for the Court to "recognize" a classification? In order to justify its authority to extend constitutional protection to certain classifications, the Court has developed standards of judicial review to be applied to government laws or practices. Those standards include concepts of "strict scrutiny," proper to "suspect classifications"; "rational basis review," proper to "non-suspect classifications"; or indeed "intermediary scrutiny," proper to "quasi-suspect classifications."[24] Those classifications are ascertained with reference to criteria such as membership within a "discrete and insular minority" (as has been found with certain ethnic groups); or possession of an "immutable characteristic"

---

[16] U.S. Const. amend. XIV, §1. Although the clause refers only to the States, the Supreme Court has held that the federal government is also prohibited from practicing "unjustifiable" discrimination. *Bolling v. Sharpe*, 347 U.S. 497 (1954).

[17] See chapter 2, note 3 *supra*.

[18] See, e.g., ECHR art. 14.

[19] Slaughter-House Cases, 83 U.S. (16 Wall.) 36 (1873).

[20] See Nowak and Rotunda, 2000: ch. 14.

[21] *Reed v. Reed*, 404 U.S. 71 (1971).

[22] *Graham v. Richardson*, 403 U.S. 365 (1971).

[23] *New Jersey Welfare Rights Org. v. Cahill*, 411 U.S. 619 (1973).

[24] Cf. Heinze, 2003b.

(such as skin color or some other anatomical feature); or to a group's relative "political powerlessness."[25]

In view of what appears to be the Court's painstakingly articulated jurisprudence, developed over a long period of time, does our formal model, appearing to lump US law together with that of other countries, end up blunting a precision so meticulously achieved by the Court over decades of case-by-case adjudication?   The high degree of volume and detail in US equal protection jurisprudence has resulted in a corpus particularly suited to test the accuracy of our model.

In *Cleburne v. Cleburne Living Center*,[26] the Court delivered a judgment almost entirely devoted to restating and examining its standards of review.   The claimants had challenged the respondent city government's denial of a permit for the operation of a group home for the mentally retarded.   The Court had to decide whether mental retardation should be included among classifications already recognized as "suspect" or "quasi-suspect," such as race, national origin or sex. According to the Court, government action that accords differential treatment to persons based upon these kinds of characteristics is subject to "heightened scrutiny."   This means that government must overcome a stronger presumption of unconstitutionality than that raised by differential treatment of persons not belonging to such classifications.[27]

The Court declined to recognize distinctions drawn on the basis of mental retardation as "suspect" or "quasi-suspect."   "The general rule," wrote Justice White, "is that legislation is presumed to be valid, and will be sustained if the classification drawn by the statute is rationally related to a legitimate state interest. The general rule gives way, however, when a statute classifies by race, alienage, or national origin. [...] [T]hese laws are subjected to strict scrutiny."[28]   In a separate opinion, Justice Marshall noted that "[h]eightened but not strict scrutiny is considered appropriate in areas such as gender, illegitimacy or alienage because the Court views the trait as relevant under some circumstances but not others."[29] Justice Stevens, meanwhile, wrote,

> [O]ur cases reflect a continuum ... ranging from "strict scrutiny" ... to "rational basis" .... I have never been persuaded that these so called "standards" adequately explain the decisional process. [...] [I] have always asked myself whether I could find a "rational basis" for the classification at issue. [...] We do not need to apply a special standard, or to apply "strict scrutiny," or even "heightened scrutiny," to decide such cases.[30]

---

[25] See *United States v. Carolene Products*, 304 U.S. 144, 152 n. 4 (1938). Cf. Tribe, 1988: ch. 16.

[26] 473 U.S. 432 (1985).

[27] See Tribe, 1988: ch. 16.

[28] 473 U.S. at 440.

[29] *Id.* at 469 (Marshall, concurring in the judgment in part and dissenting in part).

[30] *Id.* at 451-52 (Stevens, J., concurring).

Are White's *general rule that gives way*, Marshall's *trait relevant under some circumstances but not others*, and Stevens's *rational basis* merely three different expressions of the same standard? If not, do the standards differ because of the language they use, or simply because of the substantive results they reach? Would White manifestly have reached different conclusions using Marshall's *circumstances* test? Would Marshall have been compelled to reach different results using Stevens's *rational basis* test? In other words, could the three Justices have swapped their terms, yet maintained their respective findings? Once again, we see that questions which can arise about indeterminacy across jurisdictions are the same as those which arise within jurisdictions, and, indeed, as here, among Justices deciding a single case.

Those questions, and the lack of any clear answers to them in the Court's equal protection jurisprudence, suggest that even what appears to be a highly developed rights jurisprudence does not perforce comport greater precision. Justice Stevens specifically denies that the Court's lexicon moves beyond ordinary reasonableness (or "rational basis") concepts. He can reach that conclusion simply by expanding the concept of "rational basis," such that there would be few rational bases to justify, say, racial classifications, but a wide range of bases for defending routine legislative or administrative classifications.[31] Every case ever decided under "heightened scrutiny" could, then, have been decided under "rational basis" review, and *vice versa*, with no difference in the substantive outcome, and only nominal differences in reasoning.[32] Justice Marshall suggests as much when he confesses to "puzzling" over a Court decision which calls mental retardation a non-suspect classification, requiring only rational-basis scrutiny, but which then subjects the ordinance to "precisely the sort of probing inquiry associated with heightened scrutiny."[33]

One might, of course, raise a hard-cases-make-bad-law objection: these difficulties are to be expected in the case of such a complex issue as mental retardation. Yet even the common classifications are not immune from these problems. No sooner had the Justices recognized sex as a protected classification[34]—a classification which, unlike mental retardation, affects half the population—than they were compelled to distinguish it from other kinds of classifications.[35] A racial classification would likely have been found invalid in *Dothard*, but a sex distinction was upheld. It is for this reason that the Court has accepted "two tier" review of protected classifications, whereby classifications such as race or national origin are construed as "suspect" and entitled to "strict scrutiny",

---

[31] On routine legislative or administrative classifications, see Section 14.5 *infra*.

[32] Cf. 473 U.S. at 451 n. 2 (Stevens, J., concurring) (noting other cases in which members of the Court have expressed doubts about the determinacy of the standards of review). Cf. also *Craig v. Boren*, 429 U.S. 190, 211 (1976) (Stevens, J., concurring).

[33] 473 U.S. at 458.

[34] See *Reed v. Reed*, 404 U.S. 71 (1971).

[35] See, e.g., *Boren*, 429 U.S. 190 (1976). Cf. *id.* at 210 (Powell, J., concurring). Cf. also *id.* at 217 (Rehnquist, J., dissenting).

while sex is treated as "quasi-suspect" entitled to an intermediary level of review.[36] Other classifications, such as routine regulatory or administrative distinctions, are treated as "non-suspect," entitled only to low-level, rational-basis review.[37] In real terms, these different tiers of review merely mean that the Court is willing to defer to a broader range of "o" values in the case of sex than in the case of race. That is all that such an ostensibly intricate scheme of judicial review *can* mean. "Heightened scrutiny" can mean only greater deference to A values; "rational basis review" can mean only greater deference to Z values; "intermediary scrutiny" can mean only some level of deference between the two.

It is not that the Court is not justified in differentiating between standards of review applied to sex and those applied to race; or between those and other classifications, such as routine regulatory and administrative classifications. However, the complexity of the Court's distinctions among "suspect," "quasi-suspect" and "non-suspect" classifications, and corresponding standards of review, can only ever express those differences in imprecise terms. In terms of substantive outcome, our formal model cannot improve upon them. It only ascertains the background of formal determinacy within which these ongoing arguments and doctrines arise in the first instance. It represents the point at which formal determinacy ends and substantive argument—however determinate or indeterminate; and we need take no view on that question—begins, e.g., at the threshold of formulas such as F.14-1 and F.14-2. Still, the Justices' intractable differences raise questions about whether the determinacy of its standards of review can go much further than sheer formal structure; and whether, for all their seeming intricacy, those standards are ultimately indistinguishable from the more prosaic "reasonableness" or "proportionality" standards used by non-US courts.[38]

But let us return to our model. The dispute in *Cleburne* had arisen from a zoning ordinance which required that the claimants secure a special permit in order to lease a building in the city as a community-care home for mildly or moderately mentally retarded individuals. No such requirement existed for non-mentally retarded persons. The city defended the ordinance on several grounds. It argued, for example, that the proposal for a home inhabited by mentally retarded individuals had prompted safety concerns among local residents, thus justifying the denial of a permit.[39] On that view, the objective status of mental retardation itself—irrespective of the actual conduct of any particular, mentally retarded individual, which was not at issue in the dispute—constituted an inequality of objective status, which entailed incommensurate subjective merit with respect to the entitlement to lease the home (F.14-2). The Court, however, accepted the claimants' view that "mere negative attitudes, or fear . . . are not permissible bases for treating a home for the mentally retarded differently from apartment houses,

---

[36] Cf. Tribe, 1988: 1561-65.
[37] See, e.g., *FCC v. Beach Communications*, 508 U.S. 307 (1993).
[38] Heinze, 2003b.
[39] 473 U.S. at 448.

multiple dwellings, and the like."[40] In view of the actual individuals who would inhabit the home, and the supervision that would be provided, the Court found no "rational basis for believing that the . . . home would pose any special threat to the city's legitimate interests."[41] Thus, for purposes of inhabiting a home in the community, commensurate subjective merit of the mentally retarded—not compromised through sheer unsubstantiated fear on the part of local residents—entailed equality of objective status (F.14-1).

The city also adduced two objections in a paternalist vein. The home was located near a junior high school, and city officials feared that pupils of the school might harass the residents.[42] On that view, the objective status of mental retardation entailed a particular vulnerability, hence incommensurate subjective merit, on the part of the prospective inhabitants (F.14-2). The Court likened that fear of a special danger posed *to* residents with the fear of a special danger posed *by* them: "the school itself is attended by about 30 mentally retarded students, and denying a permit based on such vague, undifferentiated fears is again permitting some portion of the community to validate what would otherwise be an equal protection violation."[43] Deeming that fear to be groundless, then, the Court again found commensurate subjective merit on the part of the mentally retarded individuals, which entailed equality of objective status (F.14-1).

The second paternalist objection arose from the home's location on a flood plain. Here too, on the city's view, mental retardation comported a particular vulnerability, hence incommensurate subjective merit, on the part of the prospective inhabitants (F.14-2). Finding, however, that the ordinance reflected no such concern with other residential establishments in the areas, including boarding and fraternity houses, the Court concluded that the home "would present [no] different or special hazard"[44]—commensurate subjective merit in this regard, too, entailed objective equality (F.14-1).[45]

14.5 Routine Statutory and Administrative Classifications

The traditional model also encompasses claims commonly arising under routine statutory and administrative classifications. Virtually any statutory or administrative classification can comport some degree of arbitrariness, opening it up to the prospect of a discrimination claim. These disputes, too, illustrate how substantive legal distinctions which may possess an arbitrary element nevertheless fulfill the requirements of formal determinacy.

---

[40] *Id.*

[41] *Id.*

[42] *Id.* at 449.

[43] *Id.*

[44] *Id.*

[45] A final objection, concerning the size of the home and the number of residents, was argued along similar lines. See *id.* at 449-450.

In the 1949 case of *Railway Express Agency v. New York*,[46] the US Supreme Court had to decide whether the Equal Protection clause was violated by a New York City traffic regulation which provided that "[n]o person shall operate [on] any street an advertising vehicle," but which made an exception for "notices upon business delivery vehicles . . . engaged in the usual business [of] the owner."[47] The city defended the regulation as a means of promoting safety by reducing distractions to drivers and pedestrians.

A complaint was brought by a company that sold advertising space on the sides of motor vehicles. In the company's view, either an advertisement is distracting or it is not—regardless of who owns or operates the vehicle, or for what purpose. The claimant considered his vehicles to be no more distracting than any other vehicles carrying advertising. The claimant thus asserted commensurate subjective merit as a basis for objective equality between those vehicles which are, and those which are not, engaged in the usual business of the owner (F.14-1). According to the Court, however, "the fact that New York City sees fit to eliminate from traffic this kind of distraction but does not touch what may be even greater ones . . . is immaterial."[48] The Court accepted the city's decision—laden though it may have been with "theoretical inconsistencies"[49]—to classify vehicles which *are not* engaged in the usual business of the owner as objectively unequal to vehicles which *are* engaged in the usual business of the owner, for purposes of achieving its safety goals (F.14-2): "It is no requirement of equal protection that all evils of the same genus be eradicated or none at all."[50]

Under the German Basic Law, the Article 3(1) right to equal protection (*Gleichheitssatz*) has been invoked to cover a variety of cases in which a claimant alleges unfair treatment in the enjoyment of rights or benefits.[51] In a 1990 case (hereinafter the *Street Tax* case),[52] the Federal Administrative Court (*Bundesverwaltungsgericht*) held invalid the application of a Bavarian ordinance which required that landowners whose land abuts a street pay a street maintenance tax. Although the claimant's land abutted a street, it had no direct access to that street. The claimant thus complained of being treated unequally, under the ordinance, to all other persons whose property lacked direct street access, and who did not have to pay the tax.

As in *Belgian Linguistic*, this case can be understood in two formally opposed, but substantively identical ways. On one reading, the claimant complains of *equal* treatment as compared with owners of adjacent land having direct access to the street [A_i: $T^{-\gamma}$], and correlates to a normative assertion of compulsory *un*equal treatment [A_i: $\sim T^c$]. In response, the government authority asserts factual as well as normative equal treatment [Z_i: $T^{-\gamma} \cdot T^p$]. On another reading, the claimant

---

[46] 336 U.S. 106 (1949).
[47] *Id.* at 107-08.
[48] *Id.* at 110.
[49] *Id.*
[50] *Id.*
[51] Bleckmann, 1997: 644-45.
[52] 81 BVerwGE 371 (1990).

complains of *un*equal treatment as compared with other persons whose land lacks direct street access [A_{ii}: $\sim T^{\gamma} \cdot T^{c}$], the government's response being that such inequality is justified [Z_{ii}: $\sim T^{\gamma} \cdot \sim T^{p}$]. On either reading, it is not different values of τ that differentiate the two sets of θ positions. In either set, τ simply represents the imposition of the tax. What differentiates the two sets of θ positions are the respective values of o as applied to τ. Where o represents the characteristic of ownership of land without access to the street, the claimant argues that lack of access means that she maintains commensurate subjective merit for purposes of *non*-payment of the tax, and thereby objective equality to other properties lacking direct access to the street (A_{ii}, F.14-1). The government responds that the status of objective inequality with all other properties lacking direct access—insofar as those properties do not abut the street—suffices to justify a finding of incommensurate merit for purposes of *non*-payment of the tax (Z_{ii}, F.14-2). Alternatively, where o represents the characteristic of ownership of land abutting the street, the claimant argues that it is her inability to use the street in the way enjoyed by other owners of abutting properties which provides a sufficient condition for a finding of unequal objective status as an abutting property,

F.14-3 A_i: $[(T^{\gamma} \cdot \sim S \cdot \sim O) \cdot (\sim S \rightarrow \sim T^{c})] \Rightarrow B$

For the government, however, the objective status of abutment itself suffices to justify a finding of commensurate subjective merit for purposes of payment of the tax,

F.14-4 Z_i: $[(T^{\gamma} \cdot S \cdot O) \cdot (O \rightarrow T^{p})] \Rightarrow \sim B$

As in *Belgian Linguistic*, the Court does not, and need not, clearly distinguish between the θ_i and θ_{ii} positions. The two sets of arguments form part of the same rationale. By definition, the claimant's land is dissimilarly situated to other street-abutting lands precisely because it is similarly situated to properties without street access.

14.6   Affirmative Action

The US case of *Adarand Constructors v. Pena*[53] arose from a policy, adopted by a division of the United States Department of Transportation, of awarding a percentage of subcontracting jobs in contracts for federal highway construction to minority-controlled businesses. The government defended the differential treatment by noting historical inequalities between whites and non-whites with respect to their presence in the construction industry. In its view, that objective inequality effectively justified a finding of incommensurate merit on the part of the white majority (F.14-2). The Court, however, found the policy unconstitutional.

---

[53] 515 U.S. 200 (1995).

The Adarand construction company alleged that, as a result of the policy, it had failed to win a federal highway construction contract, despite having submitted a bid to complete the required work at a lower cost. The company thus asserted that it possessed commensurate ability to perform the requisite tasks, which justified a finding of objective equality of minority-owned and non-minority-owned businesses. That finding would require equal treatment (F.14-1), meaning, in this case, that the contract would have to go to the best bid.

Similar arguments have arisen in sex-based affirmative action cases. The European Communities Equal Treatment Directive prohibits sex discrimination, but "without prejudice to measures to promote equal opportunity for men and women, in particular by removing existing inequalities which affect women's opportunities." [54]   The case of *Kalanke v. Freie Hansestadt Bremen*[55] concerned a policy of preferential promotion of women by the Bremen Parks Department, in cases in which a man and a woman are equally qualified. As in *Adarand*, the policy was motivated by a finding of historical inequalities between men and women in the workplace (F.14-2). The claimant, a male employee, alleged that a woman had been promoted over him on the basis of the policy, despite his equal or superior qualification (F.14-1).   The Court construed art. 2(4) to allow "measures . . . which give a specific advantage to women with a view to improving their ability to compete in the labour market and to pursue a career on an equal footing with men."[56]   But, it continued, "[n]ational rules which guarantee women absolute and unconditional priority go beyond promoting equal opportunities and overstep the limits of the exception in Art 2(4)."[57]

Subsequently, in *Marschall v. Land Nordrhein-Westfalen*,[58] a case difficult to reconcile with *Kalanke*, the Court took a different view. *Marschall* concerned a school promotion policy which provided that where "there are fewer women than men in the particular higher grade post in the career bracket, women are to be given priority for promotion in the event of equal suitability, competence and professional performance, unless reasons specific to an individual [male] candidate tilt the balance in his favour."[59]   As in *Kalanke*, a male employee complained of non-promotion despite equal or superior qualification (F.14-1). Here, however, the Court accepted the respondent's position (F.14-2), as male candidates were, at least in principle, entitled to individualized assessments as to balance-tilting factors, whereas the policy in *Kalanke* envisaged preferential treatment for equally qualified women unconditionally.[60]   Once again, as with the US Supreme Court Justices' differing views in *Cleburne*, we see that the doubtful substantive compatibility of divergent positions in no way affects the formal criteria qualifying them as arguments in discrimination cases.

---

[54] 76/207/EEC, 1976 O.J. (L 39/40), art. 2(4).
[55] Case 450/93, 1995 E.C.R. 3051.
[56] *Id.* at 3077.
[57] *Id.* at 3078.
[58] Case 409/95, 1997 E.C.R. 6363.
[59] *Id.* at 6386.
[60] *Id.* at 6392-93.

14.7   Hard Cases

Indeed, *Kalanke* and *Marschall* are not the only examples of less-than-coherent affirmative action jurisprudence. The foregoing analysis of *Adarand* might leave the impression that the arguments in that case were clear-cut; but that was hardly the case. *Adarand* resulted from a two-decade struggle with affirmative action which had produced a tortuous, arguably internally contradictory, line of cases. It might appear that a reduction of *Adarand* to a dichotomy of two mutually exclusive alternatives—*either* the A position *or* the Z position—fails to reflect the labyrinthine path traced by the Court in the series of cases that led up to it. So let us take a closer look at those cases, in order to consider a question which concerns not just affirmative action, but the entire enterprise of judicial resolution of controversial issues. How can our strictly bi-polar model account for the ruffled edges and gray areas of an intricate body of case law?

The 1978 case of *University of California v. Bakke*[61] involved a challenge to a university affirmative action policy, under which places were reserved for ethnic minority applicants. In an opinion written by Justice Powell, the Court found the policy discriminatory, but reached that conclusion on the narrow grounds that the policy fixed an express quota of 16 out of 100 places.[62] Justices Brennan, White, Marshall and Blackmun joined Justice Powell—hence a five-Justice majority—in expressing the view that a more flexible policy would be constitutional *on substantive grounds*: these included demonstrable histories and ongoing practices of racial discrimination, as well as a public interest in promoting social and educational diversity.[63]

Two years later, in *Fullilove v. Klutznick*,[64] the Court upheld a federal minority set-aside program, which provided a limited preference for minority owned and operated businesses for certain public building projects. However, there was no longer a majority of Justices willing to do so on those same substantive grounds. Instead, Chief Justice Burger's plurality opinion cited rather narrower considerations of federalism, arguing that the federal program merited judicial deference, insofar as Section 5 of the Fourteenth Amendment[65] expressly authorizes Congress to enforce the provisions of the Equal Protection Clause,[66] thus leaving open the possibility that an identical program adopted by a State or local government, on identical substantive grounds, could be found unconstitutional.

That possibility materialized in *Richmond v. J.A. Croson Co.*,[67] in which the Court struck down a local minority set-aside program. In that case, and then even further in *Adarand*, the Court's plurality opinion attempted to confine the scope of

---

[61] 438 U.S. 265 (1978)
[62] *Id.* at 316.
[63] *Id.* at 316-18. See also *id.* at 324 (Brennan, J., concurring in the judgment in part and dissenting) (joined by White, Marshall and Blackmun, JJ.).
[64] 448 U.S. 448 (1980).
[65] U.S. Const. amend. XIV, §5.
[66] 448 U.S. at 472.
[67] 488 U.S. 479 (1989)

Fullilove to the narrowest considerations of federalism. More recently, the Supreme Court has declined to hear—raising the question of its tacit approval of—an appeal from a judgment of a federal circuit court that had rejected the kind of flexible university affirmative action admissions program which the five Justices had endorsed in *Bakke*, categorically finding that race-based preferences were "per se proscribed."[68] The ultimate question, then, of whether any kind of affirmative action program can now survive scrutiny by the Court, and on what grounds that decision would be reached, remains unclear.

Our formal model does not expressly record casuistic differentials at that level of precision. That is not its purpose. As we have seen with *Cleburne, Kalanke* and *Marschall*, its purpose is merely to situate the doctrinal complexity of disputes, insofar as that is possible, within a fixed, formal framework. Thus, in these cases, insofar as the Court finds some form of affirmative action constitutional, it does so by accepting the "o" values adduced in the Z position (F.14-2), regardless of the Justices' doctrinal reasons for doing so—that is, regardless of whether they do so on substantive grounds, or on narrower grounds of federalism. Insofar as the Court finds some form of affirmative action to be *un*constitutional—and even if it should ultimately find all such programs unconstitutional—it does so by accepting the σ values adduced in the A position (F.14-1), but, again, regardless of its doctrinal reasons for doing so, and even if those doctrinal reasons expressly contradict (or overrule) those which a majority of its members had earlier accepted.

Exercise Set 14-1

From the following arguments, derive the general formula
A: $[(\tau^{-\gamma} \cdot \sigma \cdot o) \cdot (\sigma \to \tau^c)] \Rightarrow B$

1. A: $[(\sim T^{-\gamma} \cdot S \cdot O) \cdot (S \to T^c)] \Rightarrow B$
2. A: $[(T^{-\gamma} \cdot \sim S \cdot \sim O) \cdot (\sim S \to \sim T^c)] \Rightarrow B$

Exercise Set 14-2

From the following arguments, derive the general formula
Z: $[(\tau^{-\gamma} \cdot \sigma \cdot o) \cdot (o \to \tau^p)] \Rightarrow \sim B$

1. Z: $[(\sim T^{-\gamma} \cdot \sim S \cdot \sim O) \cdot (\sim O \to \sim T^p)] \Rightarrow \sim B$
2. Z: $[(T^{-\gamma} \cdot S \cdot O) \cdot (O \to T^p)] \Rightarrow \sim B$

---

[68] *Hopwood v. Texas*, 78 F.3d 932 (5th Cir.1996), *cert. denied*, 518 U.S. 1033 (1996).

Answers to Exercises

Exercise Set 14-1

1. (1)   A: $[(\sim T^{\gamma} \cdot S \cdot O) \cdot (S \to T^c)] \Rightarrow B$ given
   (2)   A: $[(\tau^{\gamma} \cdot S \cdot O) \cdot (S \to T^c)] \Rightarrow B$ Ps(τ^{γ})
   (3)   A: $[(\tau^{\gamma} \cdot \sigma \cdot O) \cdot (\sigma \to T^c)] \Rightarrow B$ Ps(σ)
   (4)   A: $[(\tau^{\gamma} \cdot \sigma \cdot o) \cdot (\sigma \to T^c)] \Rightarrow B$ Ps(o)
   ∴   A: $[(\tau^{\gamma} \cdot \sigma \cdot o) \cdot (\sigma \to \tau^c)] \Rightarrow B$ Ps(τ^c)

2. (1)   A: $[(T^{\gamma} \cdot \sim S \cdot \sim O) \cdot (\sim S \to \sim T^c)] \Rightarrow B$ given
   (2)   A: $[(\tau^{\gamma} \cdot \sim S \cdot \sim O) \cdot (\sim S \to \sim T^c)] \Rightarrow B$ Ps(τ^{γ})
   (3)   A: $[(\tau^{\gamma} \cdot \sigma \cdot \sim O) \cdot (\sigma \to T^c)] \Rightarrow B$ Ps(σ)
   (4)   A: $[(\tau^{\gamma} \cdot \sigma \cdot o) \cdot (\sigma \to T^c)] \Rightarrow B$ Ps(o)
   ∴   A: $[(\tau^{\gamma} \cdot \sigma \cdot o) \cdot (\sigma \to \tau^c)] \Rightarrow B$ Ps(τ^c)

Exercise Set 14-2

1. (1)   Z: $[(\sim T^{\gamma} \cdot \sim S \cdot \sim O) \cdot (\sim O \to \sim T^p)] \Rightarrow \sim B$ given
   (2)   Z: $[(\tau^{\gamma} \cdot \sim S \cdot \sim O) \cdot (\sim O \to \sim T^p)] \Rightarrow \sim B$ Ps(τ^{γ})
   (3)   Z: $[(\tau^{\gamma} \cdot \sigma \cdot \sim O) \cdot (\sigma \to \sim T^p)] \Rightarrow \sim B$ Ps(σ)
   (4)   Z: $[(\tau^{\gamma} \cdot \sigma \cdot o) \cdot (\sigma \to \sim T^p)] \Rightarrow \sim B$ Ps(o)
   ∴   Z: $[(\tau^{\gamma} \cdot \sigma \cdot o) \cdot (o \to \tau^p)] \Rightarrow \sim B$ Ps(τ^p)

2. (1)   Z: $[(T^{\gamma} \cdot S \cdot O) \cdot (O \to T^p)] \Rightarrow \sim B$ given
   (2)   Z: $[(\tau^{\gamma} \cdot S \cdot O) \cdot (O \to T^p)] \Rightarrow \sim B$ Ps(τ^{γ})
   (3)   Z: $[(\tau^{\gamma} \cdot \sigma \cdot O) \cdot (\sigma \to \sim T^p)] \Rightarrow \sim B$ Ps(σ)
   (4)   Z: $[(\tau^{\gamma} \cdot \sigma \cdot o) \cdot (\sigma \to \sim T^p)] \Rightarrow \sim B$ Ps(o)
   ∴   Z: $[(\tau^{\gamma} \cdot \sigma \cdot o) \cdot (o \to \tau^p)] \Rightarrow \sim B$ Ps(τ^p)

15 The Impact Model

Unlike the Traditional Model, the remaining models in this book reflect more specialized issues. In this chapter, we examine arguments arising from claims that policies or practices are discriminatory in effect regardless of the presence or absence of discriminatory intent.

15.1 General Form

Like the traditional model, the claimant's argument in the *impact model* is premised on a claim about subjective merit. In response, however, the respondent's argument is premised not on an assumption about objective inequality, but rather on a *contrary* assumption about subjective merit. That is, the entire dispute is about the value of σ,

$$A: [(\tau^{-\gamma} \cdot \sigma \cdot o) \cdot (\sigma \to \tau^c)] \Rightarrow B$$

$$Z: [(\tau^{-\gamma} \cdot \sigma \cdot o) \cdot (\sigma \to \tau^p)] \Rightarrow {\sim}B$$

15.2 Discriminatory Impact

Since the mid-20th century, there have been increasing numbers of claims alleging discriminatory *impact*. In these claims, it is asserted that, even if the respondent did not intend to discriminate, its policies or practices have had a discriminatory effect, by unduly disadvantaging some sector of the population.[1] For example, the EU case of *Gerster v. Freistaat Bayern*[2] concerned the legality of an employment policy which excluded part-time work from the calculation of total time served for purposes of promotions. Despite the policy's *prima facie* neutrality, the claimant alleged that it in fact discriminated against women, who constituted 87% of the relevant part-time workforce.[3] The claimant noted that full-time hours do not necessarily produce greater quality of experience or expertise.[4] In her view, accepted by the Court, women's commensurate subjective merit resulted in objective equality of men and women for purposes of seeking promotions. The

---

[1] Cf. Townshend-Smith 1998: ch. 9; Zimmer *et al.*. 1997: chs. 5, 6.

[2] Case 1/95, 1997 E.C.R. 5253.

[3] *Id.* at 5264.

[4] *Id.* at 5286.

disqualification of part-time work thus amounted to a form of unequal—even if unintentional—treatment,

F.15-1   A: $[(\sim T^{\gamma} \cdot S \cdot O) \cdot (S \to T^{c})] \Rightarrow B$

The Bavarian government defended the policy by arguing that part-time work results in a lower level of experience;[5] a lower level of experience entails incommensurate subjective merit, thus justifying any objective inequality of impact on the sexes,

Z: $[(\sim S \to \sim O) \cdot (\sim O \to \sim T^{p})] \Rightarrow (\sim S \to \sim T^{p})$

Hence,

F.15-2   Z: $[(\sim T^{\gamma} \cdot \sim S \cdot \sim O) \cdot (\sim S \to \sim T^{p})] \Rightarrow \sim B$

Indeed, an argument alleging incommensurate substantive merit as a justification for disparate treatment would be expected in an impact case, if there truly is no policy or practice expressly based on an identified objective status.

Consider some other examples. The US case of *Wards Cove Packing Co.* v. *Atonio*[6] arose from a complaint of discrimination in the Alaskan salmon canning industry. Jobs at the canneries were of two general kinds. Many unskilled "cannery jobs" were held by Filipinos and indigenous Alaskans. By contrast, the better paid "noncannery jobs," which were generally skilled positions, were held mostly by whites. A group of cannery workers brought the complaint, alleging that the canneries' hiring practices for noncannery positions discriminated against non-whites. For example, in one round of hiring, only 17% of new hires for medical jobs, and only 15% of new hires for office jobs, were non-white, despite a non-white workforce of 52% in the cannery positions. The claimants alleged that, even if without intent, the hiring practices were such as to favor whites over non-whites for the noncannery jobs. The result was that potentially qualified non-whites were passed over in favor of whites (F.15-1). Here too, the respondents did not, as under the traditional model, assert any inequality of non-whites as such as disposing of the question of qualification, but just the opposite. On their view, which the Court accepted, it was lack of qualification, hence incommensurate subjective merit, which justified any resulting inequality between whites and non-whites (F.15-2).

A number of claims have been brought in Swiss cantons involving complaints of discrimination in fire fighting departments.[7] Preferential hiring of men has been defended, in part, on the basis of *prima facie* neutral criteria of comparatively greater physical size of men (F.15-2). However, an increasing acceptance of the

[5] *Id.*
[6] 490 U.S. 642 (1989).
[7] Müller, 1999: 445-46.

equal ability of women to perform the requisite functions (F.15-1) has resulted in successful constitutional challenges to such restrictions.

Exercise Set 15-1

1. *From the argument* A: $[(\sim T^{\gamma} \cdot S \cdot O) \cdot (S \to T^c)] \Rightarrow B$ *derive the general formula* A: $[(\tau^{\gamma} \cdot \sigma \cdot o) \cdot (\sigma \to \tau^c)] \Rightarrow B$.

2. *From the argument* Z: $[(\sim T^{\gamma} \cdot \sim S \cdot \sim O) \cdot (\sim S \to T^p)] \Rightarrow \sim B$ *derive the general formula* Z: $[(\tau^{\gamma} \cdot \sigma \cdot o) \cdot (\sigma \to \tau^p)] \Rightarrow \sim B$.

Answers to Exercises

Exercise Set 15-1

1. (1) A: $[(\sim T^{\gamma} \cdot S \cdot O) \cdot (S \to T^c)] \Rightarrow B$ given
   (2) A: $[(\tau^{\gamma} \cdot \sim S \cdot \sim O) \cdot (\sim S \to T^c)] \Rightarrow \sim B$ Ps(τ^{γ})
   (3) A: $[(\tau^{\gamma} \cdot \sigma \cdot \sim O) \cdot (\sigma \to T^c)] \Rightarrow \sim B$ Ps(σ)
   (4) A: $[(\tau^{\gamma} \cdot \sigma \cdot o) \cdot (\sigma \to T^c)] \Rightarrow \sim B$ Ps(o)
   $\therefore$ A: $[(\tau^{\gamma} \cdot \sigma \cdot o) \cdot (\sigma \to \tau^c)] \Rightarrow \sim B$ Ps(τ^c)

2. (1) Z: $[(\sim T^{\gamma} \cdot \sim S \cdot \sim O) \cdot (\sim S \to T^p)] \Rightarrow \sim B$ given
   (2) Z: $[(\tau^{\gamma} \cdot \sim S \cdot \sim O) \cdot (\sim S \to T^p)] \Rightarrow \sim B$ Ps(τ^{γ})
   (3) Z: $[(\tau^{\gamma} \cdot \sigma \cdot \sim O) \cdot (\sigma \to T^p)] \Rightarrow \sim B$ Ps(σ)
   (4) Z: $[(\tau^{\gamma} \cdot \sigma \cdot o) \cdot (\sigma \to T^p)] \Rightarrow \sim B$ Ps(o)
   $\therefore$ Z: $[(\tau^{\gamma} \cdot \sigma \cdot o) \cdot (\sigma \to \tau^p)] \Rightarrow \sim B$ Ps(τ^c)

16 The Accommodation Model

In this chapter we examine another more specialized type of claim, namely, that discrimination has resulted from a failure to take adequate steps to accommodate an individual's particular needs or circumstances.

16.1 General Form

In the *accommodation model*, the places of σ and o are the reverse of the traditional model. Now it is the claimant whose arguments about subjective merit derive from some generalized view about his or her objective status, while the respondent replies by drawing upon an individualized assertion about the claimant's subjective merit,

A: $[(\tau^{-\gamma} \cdot \sigma \cdot o) \cdot (o \to \tau^c)] \Rightarrow B$

Z: $[(\tau^{-\gamma} \cdot \sigma \cdot o) \cdot (\sigma \to \tau^p)] \Rightarrow {\sim}B$

16.2 Disability

The accommodation model is common in cases where claimants assert particular subjective needs, based on their objective status. The respondent justifies the failure to accommodate those needs by adopting a contrary view as to the nature or gravity of the subjective need. This scenario is arising increasingly in the context of disability. As noted in one study, "some individuals may be qualified to work, but only if the employer accommodates their disability in some way. These individuals, unlike most other statutorily protected groups, require some form of accommodation or different treatment in order to enjoy equal access to employment opportunities and benefits."[1]

In *Vande Zande v. State of Wisconsin Department of Administration*,[2] a woman complained about her employer's failure, under the Americans with Disabilities Act,[3] to accommodate her partial physical paralysis. It was agreed that certain accommodation had already been made by the respondent. What remained in dispute were certain additional requests by the claimant which the employer had

---

[1] Zimmer *et al.*, 1997: 824.
[2] 44 F.3d 538 (7th Cir. 1995).
[3] 42 U.S.C. §§ 12101 *et seq.* (1990).

refused to meet. As to the disputed accommodation, then, the employee, as a formal matter, complained not about being treated *un*equally to non-disabled employees, but of merely being treated equally to them. In such a case, the disability is asserted as an unequal objective status in comparison with the non-disabled status of other employees, justifying a finding of subjective need significantly greater than—and in that sense incommensurate with—the needs of other employees,

$$A: [(\sim O \rightarrow \sim S) \cdot (\sim S \rightarrow \sim T^c)] \Rightarrow (\sim O \rightarrow \sim T^c)$$

Hence,

$$F.16\text{-}1 \quad A: [(T^{\sim \gamma} \cdot \sim S \cdot \sim O) \cdot (\sim O \rightarrow \sim T^c)] \Rightarrow B$$

The respondent refused to provide the further accommodations on the grounds that to do so would have imposed considerable additional expense, while only slightly increasing the claimant's productivity or comfort. Up to a point, then, reasonable accommodation had already been provided. Beyond that point, the employer felt justified in refusing the employee's further requests—i.e., in assuming no more than commensurate (as opposed to special) need on the employee's part, as a basis for treating the disabled employee equally to non-disabled employees,

$$Z: [(S \rightarrow O) \cdot (O \rightarrow T^p)] \Rightarrow (S \rightarrow T^p)$$

Hence,

$$F.16\text{-}2 \quad Z: [(T^{\sim \gamma} \cdot S \cdot O) \cdot (S \rightarrow T^p)] \Rightarrow \sim B$$

16.3 Religion

Non-discrimination norms in contemporary human rights instruments commonly include enumerated lists of protected classifications, such as race, ethnicity or sex.[4] One of the most commonly included classifications is religion. However, in addition to the inclusion of religion as a protected classification under the non-discrimination norm, contemporary individual rights instruments usually include distinct rights of religious freedom.[5] For example, article 14 of the European Convention includes religion among its expressly protected classifications, such that Convention rights are to be enjoyed by all individuals regardless of their religion; however, standing alone, that right could be construed to provide only a

---

[4] See UDHR art. 2; ICCPR arts. 2, 26. Cf. Section 14.4, text accompanying note 18 *supra*.
[5] See, e.g., UDHR art. 18; ICCPR art. 18.

minimum of protection, allowing a State to impose heavy restrictions on religious freedom as long as it did so equally with respect to all religions. Accordingly, article 9 provides, as a distinct matter, that "[e]veryone has the right to freedom of . . . religion," as an assurance of some meaningful minimum of substantive protection.

Indeed, it might be argued that the inclusion of religion in article 14 is redundant, as the protections of article 9 should provide at least equal, if not greater, protection from any incursion on religious interests. The jurisprudence of the US Bill of Rights might be cited as an illustration. The Free Exercise clause of the First Amendment provides that "Congress shall make no law . . . prohibiting the free exercise" of religion.[6] As the Supreme Court has generally applied that provision to resolve complaints of unfair treatment on grounds of religion, it has not had to incorporate religion into its Equal Protection jurisprudence. Yet the case law leaves unresolved the question whether the Free Exercise clause provides additional protection, or is indeed nothing more than an Equal Protection clause for religion.[7] The question thus remains whether equal protection principles are a "floor" or a "ceiling" for Free Exercise jurisprudence: is equal treatment on the basis of religion the least, or the most, that government must provide under Free Exercise clause? As with the other models, substantive disagreements do not preclude a formally determinate stucture.

The case of *Bowen v. Roy*[8] arose when Native American claimants were denied social welfare benefits for their child, after having refused, on religious grounds, to provide a social security number for the child. In a plurality opinion, three Justices appeared willing to go no further than a "ceiling" requirement. They maintained that the assignment of a social security number could be imposed as a condition for receiving welfare benefits, as long as the government could demonstrate that it imposed that condition in a "neutral and uniform" way, which did not expressly target any religion.[9] In a separate opinion, Justice O'Connor rejected that position: "[s]uch a test . . . relegates a serious First Amendment value to the barest level of minimal scrutiny that the Equal Protection Clause already provides."[10] In a case decided the next year,[11] a majority of Justices rejected the plurality opinion in *Roy*, embracing Justice O'Connor's position. Yet three years later, in *Employment Division v. Smith*, a majority of the Court revived *Roy's* plurality view.[12] In that case, the Court upheld a State prohibition on the use of peyote, classified as a controlled substance due to its risks to health, despite its ritual use in Native American religious practice. Although the Justices who

---

[6] U.S. Const. amend. I. The provisions of the First Amendment have been held by the Court to be applicable to the States. See, e.g., Nowak and Rotunda, 2000: 368-70.

[7] Cf., with respect to the Establishment Clause, *Mitchell v. Helms*, 530 U.S. 793 (2000).

[8] 476 U.S. 693 (1986).

[9] 476 U.S. 693, 707-08 (1986) (Burger, C.J., joined by Powell and Rehnquist, JJ.).

[10] *Id.* at 724 (O'Connor, J., concurring in part and dissenting in part, joined by Brennan and Marshall, JJ.).

[11] *Hobbie v. Unemployment Appeals Comm'n*, 480 U.S. 136 (1987).

[12] 494 U.S. 872 (1990).

disagreed with the majority did not entirely agree on an alternative position, they continued to share Justice O'Connor's general approach in *Roy*.[13]

In these cases, the claimants, adopting the "floor" approach, seek some affirmative accommodation of their beliefs (F.16-1): in *Roy*, an exemption from the requirement of providing a social security number; in *Smith*, an exemption from penalties imposed for drug use. The respondents adopt the "ceiling" approach, attributing only commensurate, as opposed to special, merit to the claimants, in order to justify objective equality (F.16-2).

Title VII of the United States federal Civil Rights Act of 1964[14] *does* include religion among such enumerated grounds of discrimination as race, color, sex or national origin. Yet the formal positions adduced in argument are the same. The case of *Wilson v. U.S. West Communications*[15] concerned a woman who, motivated by religious belief, had attended work wearing an anti-abortion button depicting an aborted fetus. She was dismissed on the grounds that the button had caused distress to colleagues and disturbed the workplace environment. The claimant argued that the employer was bound under Title VII to accommodate her religious beliefs (F.16-1). The court, however, found for the employer, reasoning that a dress code may be sufficiently related to the needs of a productive or congenial workplace environment as to permit an employer some discretion in setting dress standards. On this view, the employer was entitled to find that the claimant enjoyed only commensurate, and not special, merit with regard to dress, thus justifying objective equality between her and persons holding other beliefs (F.16-2).

16.4   Comparison with the Impact Model

The British case of *London Underground Ltd. v. Edwards*[16] arose from a complaint that changes to the London Underground system had had a discriminatory effect on single mothers. Ms. Edwards, a single mother with a young child, had worked as a train operator from Sundays to Fridays, on shifts from 8.00 or 8.30 in the morning to 4.00 or 4.30 in the afternoon. The Underground authorities subsequently adopted a schedule which required that employees either begin work at 4.45 in the morning, or assume longer shifts, but without additional pay.

The Underground authorities argued that 100% of male employees and 95% of female employees had not objected to the new arrangements. On that view, any objection was personal to Ms. Edwards, and concerned only her willingness to comply with routine demands of employment—a lack of willingness on her part

---

[13] See *id.* at 891 (O'Connor, J., concurring in the judgment, joined in part by Brennan, Marshall and Blackmun, JJ.). See also *id.* at 907 (Blackmun, J., dissenting, joined by Brennan and Marshall, JJ.).

[14] 42 U.S.C. §2000e-2 (1964).

[15] 58 F.3d 1337 (8th Cir. 1995).

[16] [1997] Industrial Rel. L. R. 157.

thus indicating a lack of commensurate subjective merit as compared with other male and female employees,

$$\text{F.16-3} \quad \text{Z: } [(T^{\neg\gamma} \cdot {\sim}S \cdot {\sim}O) \cdot ({\sim}S \rightarrow {\sim}T^p)] \Rightarrow {\sim}B$$

The court noted that, of the 2,044 train operators, only 21 were women. It found that the small overall number of female employees therefore cast doubt on the probative value of the statistic of 95% female approval. These arguments illustrate the similarities that would arise in Z positions under the Impact and Accommodation models, notably in the respondent's reliance on statistical evidence. However, the claimant's position places the dispute under an Accommodation framework, as she argued (successfully) that her status of single mother had to be, and could be, taken into account in the drafting of work schedules (F.16-1).

Exercise Set 16-1

1. *Derive the general formula A:* $[(\tau^{\neg\gamma} \cdot \sigma \cdot o) \cdot (o \rightarrow \tau^c)] \Rightarrow B$ *from the formula A:* $[(T^{\neg\gamma} \cdot {\sim}S \cdot {\sim}O) \cdot ({\sim}O \rightarrow {\sim}T^c)] \Rightarrow B$
2. *Derive the general formula Z:* $[(\tau^{\neg\gamma} \cdot \sigma \cdot o) \cdot (\sigma \rightarrow \tau^p)] \Rightarrow {\sim}B$ *from the formula Z:* $[(T^{\neg\gamma} \cdot S \cdot O) \cdot (S \rightarrow T^p)] \Rightarrow {\sim}B$
3. *Derive the general formula Z:* $[(\tau^{\neg\gamma} \cdot \sigma \cdot o) \cdot (\sigma \rightarrow \tau^p)] \Rightarrow {\sim}B$ *from the formula Z:* $[(T^{\neg\gamma} \cdot {\sim}S \cdot {\sim}O) \cdot ({\sim}S \rightarrow {\sim}T^p)] \Rightarrow {\sim}B$

Answers to Exercises

Exercise Set 16-1

1. (1) A: $[(T^{\neg\gamma} \cdot {\sim}S \cdot {\sim}O) \cdot ({\sim}O \rightarrow {\sim}T^c)] \Rightarrow B$ given
   (2) A: $[(\tau^{\neg\gamma} \cdot {\sim}S \cdot {\sim}O) \cdot ({\sim}O \rightarrow {\sim}T^c)] \Rightarrow B$ $\text{Ps}(\tau^{\neg\gamma})$
   (3) A: $[(\tau^{\neg\gamma} \cdot \sigma \cdot {\sim}O) \cdot (\sigma \rightarrow {\sim}T^c)] \Rightarrow B$ $\text{Ps}(\sigma)$
   (4) A: $[(\tau^{\neg\gamma} \cdot \sigma \cdot o) \cdot (\sigma \rightarrow {\sim}T^c)] \Rightarrow B$ $\text{Ps}(o)$
   ∴   A: $[(\tau^{\neg\gamma} \cdot \sigma \cdot o) \cdot (\sigma \rightarrow \tau^c)] \Rightarrow B$ $\text{Ps}(\tau^c)$

2.   (1)   Z: [(T⁻ʸ · S · O) · (S → Tᵖ)] ⇒ ~B   given
      (2)   Z: [(τ⁻ʸ · S · O) · (S → Tᵖ)] ⇒ ~B   Ps(τ⁻ʸ)
      (3)   Z: [(τ⁻ʸ · σ · O) · (σ → Tᵖ)] ⇒ ~B   Ps(σ)
      (4)   Z: [(τ⁻ʸ · σ · o) · (σ → Tᵖ)] ⇒ ~B   Ps(o)
      ∴   Z: [(τ⁻ʸ · σ · o) · (σ → τᵖ)] ⇒ ~B   Ps(τᵖ)

3.   (1)   Z: [(T⁻ʸ · ~S · ~O) · (~S → ~Tᵖ)] ⇒ ~B   given
      (2)   Z: [(τ⁻ʸ · ~S · ~O) · (~S → ~Tᵖ)] ⇒ ~B   Ps(τ⁻ʸ)
      (3)   Z: [(τ⁻ʸ · σ · ~O) · (σ → ~Tᵖ)] ⇒ ~B   Ps(σ)
      (4)   Z: [(τ⁻ʸ · σ · o) · (σ → ~Tᵖ)] ⇒ ~B   Ps(o)
      ∴   Z: [(τ⁻ʸ · σ · o) · (σ → τᵖ)] ⇒ ~B   Ps(τᵖ)

17 The Non-Recognition Model

We conclude the analysis with a brief examination of arguments which can occasionally arise concerning the very existence of a classification.

17.1 General Form

Under the accommodation model, we saw claimants arguing that their objective inequality justified a finding of incommensurate—special—merit (F.16-1). The respondent replied that the affirmative measures sought were not required (F.16-2). An alternative approach for the respondent would be to deny the very existence of the claimed objective status *as a status requiring distinct recognition*: the respondent argues that the claimant's objective status is equal by definition to the objective status of other similarly situated individuals, since it simply does not exist as a distinct objective status. The entire dispute then turns on the characterization of o,

A: $[(\tau^{-\gamma} \cdot \sigma \cdot o) \cdot (o \rightarrow \tau^{c})] \Rightarrow B$

Z: $[(\tau^{-\gamma} \cdot \sigma \cdot o) \cdot (o \rightarrow \tau^{p})] \Rightarrow {\sim}B$

Of the four models, this one is the least common in controversial cases. Nevertheless, a brief examination of it is worthwhile.

17.2 Qualification as a Distinct Status

In *Vande Zande*, an alternative argument adduced by the respondent was to deny the existence of the particular disability at issue as one possessing any distinct objective status for purposes of the relevant treatment. The respondent based that argument on the claim that the claimant's condition "[did] not fit the statutory definition of a disability."[1] To deny the existence of the claimant's asserted objective status is in effect to deny the existence of any characteristic of that status which would render it unequal to the status of other employees, and thus to deny objective inequality as a basis for finding incommensurate—i.e., special— subjective merit,

---

[1] 44 F.3d 538, 543-44 (7th Cir. 1995).

F.17-1   Z: $[(O \rightarrow S) \cdot (S \rightarrow T^p)] \Rightarrow (O \rightarrow T^p)$

Hence,

F.17-2   Z: $[(T^{\neg \gamma} \cdot S \cdot O) \cdot (O \rightarrow T^p)] \Rightarrow \sim B$

The Court dismissed that argument as a preliminary matter, by recognizing the disability, hence accepting the claimant's *prima facie* case (F.16-1), but then resolving the dispute on the question of reasonable cost (F.16-2). In *Vande Zande*, then, we see that this model arises only in a preliminary way, and not as a central argument in the case.

Exercise Set 17-1

Derive the general formula Z: $[(\tau^{\neg \gamma} \cdot \sigma \cdot o) \cdot (o \rightarrow \tau^p)] \Rightarrow \sim B$ *from the formula* Z: $[(T^{\neg \gamma} \cdot S \cdot O) \cdot (O \rightarrow T^p)] \Rightarrow \sim B$

The Non-Recognition Model completes the four general forms of argument in discrimination law. Looking back, we have seen that, even within a single regime, rights jurisprudence, far from converging on clear sets of principles, remains subject to indeterminacy. There can be no uniform approach to any one system, much less to all of them. That significant degree of divergence across systems does not, however, mean that uniformity is entirely lacking. Formal analysis has provided a means for ascertaining the extent and limits of uniformity in non-discrimination discourse both within and across regimes.

We have seen that an argument can be made in favor of or in opposition to a discrimination claim insofar as it can be stated in the form of a θ position. An argument in the adjudication of a discrimination claim is necessarily an instance of some combination of τ, o and σ entailing a β conclusion. Those symbols, and their possible inter-relationships, can occur only in a fixed range of positions, as set forth under the traditional, impact, accommodation and non-recognition models. Those formal positions represent a degree of absolute determinacy and uniformity in discrimination jurisprudence.   That thesis about the norm's determinacy itself entails a thesis about its indeterminacy: the set of substantive values ascribable to the symbols occurring in θ positions remains subject to greater or lesser degrees of indeterminacy. Questions about the relationship between *substantive* determinacy and indeterminacy are the more customary jurisprudential questions, and have not been examined in this study: the analysis in this book ends where those questions begin.

The aim of this book has been neither to embrace nor to disavow the formal structure that has been developed, but only to identify it. If the formal structure appears icy and mechanical, it is only insofar as non-discrimination law is itself icy and mechanical. If the structure is manipulable, it is only insofar as non-discrimination law is itself manipulable. If the structure limits the possibility of a genuine diversification of the ways in which fundamental human interests are submitted to legal regulation, it does so only because that limitation is inextricably built into it. The formal structure is only a messenger; it is not the message.

Answers to Exercises

Exercise Set 17-1

(1)	$Z: [(T^\gamma \cdot S \cdot O) \cdot (O \to T^p)] \Rightarrow \sim B$	given
(2)	$Z: [(\tau^\gamma \cdot S \cdot O) \cdot (O \to T^p)] \Rightarrow \sim B$	$Ps(\tau^\gamma)$
(3)	$Z: [(\tau^\gamma \cdot \sigma \cdot O) \cdot (O \to T^p)] \Rightarrow \sim B$	$Ps(\sigma)$
(4)	$Z: [(\tau^\gamma \cdot \sigma \cdot o) \cdot (o \to T^p)] \Rightarrow \sim B$	$Ps(o)$
$\therefore$	$Z: [(\tau^\gamma \cdot \sigma \cdot o) \cdot (o \to \tau^p)] \Rightarrow \sim B$	$Ps(\tau^p)$

Appendix: Symbols and Formulas

Operators
:	position
⊂	set of possible values
=	equivalence
·	conjunction ("and")
→	conditional ("If..., then...")
⇒	conclusion

Markers
γ	normative
$\sim\gamma$	factual
c	compulsory
p	permissive

Positions
A	claimant
A:	claimant's position
Z	respondent
Z:	respondent's position
θ	party
θ:	party's position

Assertions
τ	treatment
$\tau^{-\gamma}$	factual assertion about treatment
τ^{γ}	normative assertion about treatment
τ^{c}	compulsory treatment
τ^{p}	permissive treatment
T^{c}	compulsory equal treatment
$\sim T^{c}$	compulsory unequal treatment
T^{p}	permissive equal treatment
$\sim T^{p}$	permissive unequal treatment
o	objective status
O	equal objective status
$\sim$O	unequal objective status
σ	subjective merit
S	equal subjective merit
$\sim$S	unequal subjective merit
β	conclusion of breach or non-breach
B	breach
$\sim$B	non-breach

Postulates
$Ps(\theta)$	$\theta \subset A, Z$	$Ps(\tau^{\gamma})$	$\tau^{\gamma} \subset \tau^{c}, \tau^{p}$
$Ps(\tau_1)$	$\tau \subset T, \sim T$	$Ps(\tau^{-\gamma})$	$\tau^{-\gamma} \subset T^{-\gamma}, \sim T^{-\gamma}$
$Ps(\tau^{c})$	$\tau^{c} \subset T^{c}, \sim T^{c}$	$Ps(\tau_2)$	$\tau \subset \tau^{\gamma}, \tau^{-\gamma}$
$Ps(\tau^{p})$	$\tau^{p} \subset T^{p}, \sim T^{p}$	$Ps(o)$	$o \subset O, \sim O$
$Ps(\gamma)$	$\gamma \subset c, p$	$Ps(\sigma)$	$\sigma \subset S, \sim S$

Theorems
$Th(\tau^{\gamma})$	$\tau^{\gamma} \subset T^{c}, \sim T^{c}, T^{p}, \sim T^{p}$
$Th(\tau)$	$\tau \subset T^{c}, \sim T^{c}, T^{p}, \sim T^{p}, T^{-\gamma}, \sim T^{-\gamma}$

Works Cited

Aristotle, 1941a, *Nicomachean Ethics*, in Richard McKeon, ed., E.M. Edghill *et al.*, trans., *The Basic Works of Aristotle*, New York: Random House.

Banton, Michael, 1999, "Discrimination Entails Comparison," in Titia Loenen and Peter Rodriquez, eds., *Non-Discrimination Law: Comparative Perspectives*, The Hague: Martinus Nijhoff, pp. 107-117.

Bleckmann, Albert, 1997, *Staatsrecht II—Die Grundrechte*, 4ᵗʰ ed., Cologne: Carl Heymanns.

Carnap, Rudolph, 1958, *Introduction to Symbolic Logic and its Applications*, W. H. Meyer and J. Wilkinson, trans., 1958, New York: Dover.

Cotterrell, Roger, 1989, *The Politics of Jurisprudence*, London: Butterworths.

Detlefsen, Michael *et al.*, 1999, *Logic from A to Z*, London: Routledge.

Dijk P. van and G.J.H van Hoof, 1998, *Theory and Practice of the European Convention on Human Rights*, 3ʳᵈ ed., The Hague: Kluwer Law International.

Dworkin, Ronald, 1986, *Law's Empire*, London: Fontana.

___, 1977, *Taking Rights Seriously*, London: Duckworth.

Fletcher, George, 1996, *Basic Concepts of Legal Thought*, Oxford: Oxford University Press.

Grayling, A.C., 1997, *An Introduction to Philosophical Logic*, 3ʳᵈ ed., Oxford: Blackwell.

Grice, H. Paul, 1975, "Logic and Conversation," in Peter Cole and Jerry L. Morgan, eds., *Syntax and Semantics*, Vol. 3, pp. 41-58 [reprinted in A.P. Martinich, ed., *The Philosophy of Language*, 3ʳᵈ ed., Oxford: Oxford University Press, ch. 11].

Guttenplan, Samuel, 1997, *The Languages of Logic*, 2ⁿᵈ ed., Oxford: Blackwell.

Harris, D.J., M. O'Boyle and C. Warbrick, 1995, *Law of the European Convention on Human Rights*, London: Butterworths.

Hart, H.L.A., 1961, *The Concept of Law*, Oxford: Oxford University Press.

Heinze, Eric, 2004, *The Logic of Constitutional Rights*, Ann Arbor: University of Michigan Press (forthcoming).

___, 2003a, *The Logic of Liberal Rights*, London: Routledge.

___, 2003b, "The Logic of Judicial Review: A Deontic Analysis," *Vermont Law Review*, Vol. 28 (forthcoming).

___, 2001, "Sexual Orientation and International Law: A Study in the Manufacture of Cross-Cultural 'Sensitivity'," *Michigan Journal of International Law*, Vol. 22, pp. 1-27.

___, 2000, Review of Elias Kastanas, *Unité et diversité: notions autonomes et marge d'appréciation des Etats dans la jurisprudence de la Cour européenne des droits de l'homme*, in *Modern Law Review*, Vol. 63, pp. 155-58.

___, 1999a, "Principles for a Meta-Discourse of Liberal Rights: The Example of the European Convention on Human Rights," *Indiana International and Comparative Law Review*, Vol. 9, pp. 319-394.

___, 1999b, "The Construction and Contingency of the Minority Concept," in D. Fottrell and B. Bowring, eds., *Minority and Group Rights in the New Millennium*, The Hague: Martinus Nijhoff.

___, 1998, "Victimless Crimes," *in Encyclopedia of Applied Ethics*, Vol. 4, pp. 463-75.

___, 1994, "Equality: Between Hegemony and Subsidiarity," *Rev. Int'l. Comm'n Jurists*, No. 52, pp. 56-65.

Henkin, Louis, 1990, *The Age of Rights*, New York: Columbia.

Heringa, Aalt, 1999, "Standards of Review for Discrimination: The Scope of Review by the Courts," in Titia Loenen and Peter Rodriquez, eds., *Non-Discrimination Law: Comparative Perspectives*, The Hague: Martinus Nijhoff, pp. 25- 37.

Hohfeld, Wesley N., 1946, *Fundamental Legal Conceptions as Applied in Judicial Reasoning*, New Haven: Yale University Press [re-published in an edition by David Campbell and Philip Thomas, eds., 2001, Aldershot: Ashgate].

Kalinowski, Georges, 1972, *La Logique des normes*, Paris: Presses Universitaires de France.

Kelsen, Hans, 1960, *Reine Rechtslehre*, 2nd ed., Vienna: Franz Deuticke.

Kelman, Mark, 1987, *A Guide to Critical Legal Studies*, Cambridge, MA: Harvard University Press.

Meier, Christian, 2000, *Der Denkweg der Juristen*, Münster: LIT Verlag.

Müller, Jörg Paul, 1999, *Grundrechte in der Schweiz*, 3rd ed., Bern: Stämpfli.

Nowak, John E. and Ronald Rotunda, 2000, Constitutional Law, 6th ed., St. Paul: West.

Rawls, John, 1999, *A Theory of Justice*, 2nd ed., Oxford: Oxford University Press.

Read, Stephen, 1995, *Thinking about Logic*, Oxford: Oxford University Press.

Robertson, A.H. and J.G. Merrills, 1996, *Human Rights in the World*, 4th ed., Manchester: Manchester University Press.

Rodes, Robert E. and Howard Pospesel, 1997, *Premises and Conclusions: Symbolic Logic for Legal Analysis*, Upper Saddle River, N.J.: Prentice Hall.

Sainsbury, Mark, 1991, *Logical Forms*, Oxford: Blackwell.

Saunders, Kevin W., 1990, "A Formal Analysis of Hohfeldian Relations," *Akron Law Review*, Vol. 23, pp. 465-506.

Simmonds, Nigel E., "Introduction," in Wesley N. Hohfeld, *Fundamental Legal Conceptions as Applied in Judicial Reasoning*, 2001, Aldershot: Ashgate, pp. ix-xxix.

Soeteman, Arend, 1989, *Logic in Law*, Dordrecht: Kluwer.

Steiner, Henry J. and Philip Alston, 2000, *International Human Rights in Context*, 2nd ed., Oxford: Oxford University Press.

Sumner, L.W., 1987, *The Moral Foundation of Rights*, Oxford: Oxford University Press.

Townshend-Smith, Richard J., 1998, *Discrimination Law*, London: Cavendish.

Tribe, Laurence, 1988, *American Constitutional Law*, 2nd ed., New York: Foundation Press.

Vierdag, E.W., 1973, *The Concept of Discrimination in International Law*, The Hague: Martinus Nijhoff.

von Wright, Georg Henrik, 1963, *Norm and Action*, London: Routledge and Kegan Paul.

___, 1951, 'Deontic Logic', *Mind*, Vol. 60, pp. 1-15 [reprinted in G.H. von Wright, 1957, *Logical Studies*], London: Routledge, pp. 58-74.

Zimmer, Michael, J., Charles A. Sullivan and Rebecca Hanner White, 1997, *Cases and Materials on Employment Discrimination*, 4th ed., New York: Aspen.

Index of Cases, Names and Topics

social welfare, *see* welfare benefits
stare decisis 11
statutory and administrative classifications
   119-21
"Street Tax" case 120-21
substitution, *see* hierarchy and substitution
suspect classifications, *see* judicial
   review
Sutherland v. United Kingdom 114-15
syllogism
   hypothetical 33 n. 9
   modus ponens 90-91

theorems 39-40
traditional model 111-24, 126, 129

translation (between ordinary and symbolic
   language) 15

*United States Dept. of Agriculture v.
   Moreno* 59, 60, 65, 67, 78-80, 81, 92,
   93, 95, 96, 100, 105, 111
University of California v. Bakke 123
unspecified markers, *see* markers,
   unspecified

*Vande Zande v. Wisconsin Dept. of
   Administration* 129, 130, 135-36

Wards Cove Packing Co. v. Atonio 127
welfare benefits 58-59, 78-80, 92, 95